ESSAYS ON
ECONOMIC LIBERALISATION AND REFORMS

ESSAYS ON ECONOMIC LIBERALISATION AND REFORMS

Prof. B. Satyanarayan

ANMOL PUBLICATIONS PVT. LTD.
NEW DELHI - 110 002 (INDIA)

ANMOL PUBLICATIONS PVT. LTD.
H.O.: 4374/4B, Ansari Road, Daryaganj,
New Delhi-110 002 (India)
Ph.: 23278000, 23261597
B.O.: No. 1015, Ist Main Road, BSK IIIrd Stage
IIIrd Phase, IIIrd Block,
Bangalore - 560 085 (India)
Visit us at: www.anmolpublications.com

Essays on Economic Liberalisation and Reforms

First Edition, 2009
ISBN 978-81-261-3781-7

PRINTED IN INDIA

Printed at Balaji Offset Press, Delhi.

Contents

Foreword

It gives me great pleasure to write the foreword to this work of Prof. B. Satyanarayan, who is presently working as Chairman, Andhra Pradesh State Finance Commission.

Prof. Satyanarayan has had a distinguished academic career spanning more than four decades. He has held many important academic positions including Head, Department of Economics at Osmania University, Hyderabad.

He has kept a lively interest in pursuing research activities. Besides being a good teacher, he has published extensively in several professional journals. He has to his credit more than a dozen books on various aspects of trade and development economics. Within economics, his primary interest has been in the two areas of trade and development. He has successfully completed a number of research projects sponsored by the University Grants Commission, Indian Council of Social Science Research and Planning Commission. He has also participated in a number of conferences. He has served on the Governing Boards of a number of research institutes. The author has thus a rich background which makes his contributions valuable.

Dr. C. Rangarajan,
Chairman Economic Advisory Council to the Prime Minister

Vigyan Bhawan Annexe, 'E' Hall,
Maulana Azad Road,
New Delhi—110011

Preface

The list of claimants of my gratitude is a long one. Dr.C. Rangarajan, Chairman, Economic Advisory Council to the Prime Minister of India, Government of India in spite of his busy schedule and heavy commitments has kindly agreed to write the Foreword of this Book. This only shows that he has a soft corner for me. The Anmol Publications Pvt. Ltd., New Delhi deserve my thanks for having accepted to publish all my papers including Book Reviews (both published and unpublished) in the form of a Book (2 Volumes) in spite of a time consuming process.

This work brings together my research papers on three related themes viz., (1) "International Economics and Trade; (2) Planning and Development Economics; and (3) Indian and Andhra Pradesh Economies" and other related themes. They were written on different occasions over a period of more than four decades while I worked at The Indian Institute of Economics, A.U. Evening College and at the Osmania University, Hyderabad.

As a matter of fact, this idea of publishing all my papers arose while I was browsing in the Library of Research and Information System for Developing Countries, New Delhi along with my Research Student Dr. B. Appa Rao. We came across all the published articles in a bound volume of Dr. V.R. Panchamukhi, its Former Director. My Research Student proposed that I should do a similar exercise atleast for the sake of posterity. I reluctantly agreed for the proposal because the written papers were lying in a pell-mell condition and is a Herculean task to put them together in a chronological manner. But somehow, I was helped by Mr. N. Radha Krishna, PA to Chairman, A.P. State Finance Commission and Dr. P. Satyanarayana, Department of Economics, Osmania University, Hyderabad for nearly two months although some of the papers are not traceable. The Anmol Publications Pvt. Ltd., New Delhi have readily accepted to publish all these papers in the form a Book. I am beholden to all of them.

I hope that this work will be useful for Policy-Makers at all levels viz., Administrators, Teachers, Researchers and Students at large. If it is so, I feel honoured.

Prof. B. Satyanarayan

Hyderabad - 500 029
(India)

Chairman
A.P. State Finance Commission

1

India and China—A Comparison of Their Planning Process*

The history of social and economic development of India and China differ in many respects. The cultural experience of India has its own uniqueness in its historical framework and the same could be claimed for China too. Recently, the East Asian record of development has attracted world attention. In the wake of its New Economic Policy, India can take some useful lessons from the Chinese production and trade scenario. This paper makes an attempt to make a relative comparison of economic development experienced by China and India, ever since they launched upon their planning process in early fifties. Since both the economies are having huge domestic markets, global attention on India and China is natural.

The Chinese Economy

The Chinese economy is characterised by an unusually large share of industry in total gross output value and, as in all the communist economies, an unusually underdeveloped services sector, reflecting the priorities of Soviet-style economic planning since the 1950's. Investment has typically taken a large share of demand, although it has not always been

* Also appeared in *Economic Growth and Social Change*, March-April, 1997.

allocated efficiently or productively. China is a poor country with GDP per head of $322 in 1990. Life expectancy, nutritional standards, and the availability of primary education nevertheless place it on par with many middle-income countries.

The resource endowment is limited and the population large: cultivable land per person is only 0.1 sq. km; mineral resources and other raw materials are concentrated far from the centres of demand; the transport network is underdeveloped; and the infrastructure is outdated. In addition, there have been periods of economic disruption brought about by irrational policies and political turmoil.

Nevertheless, real national income per head grew by an annual average of 4% during 1952-82 and by 6.8% in 1979-84, accelerated by the effects of reform policies on agriculture in particular. GDP climbed by an impressive yearly average of 9.4% in real terms during the period 1980-91.

Agriculture, whose share of gross value of industrial and agricultural output (including forestry, fishing and animal husbandry) (GVAO) was 22.4% in 1991 and whose share of GNP was then 26.6%, still plays a dominant role in terms of employment, accounting for 59.8% of the social labour force at the end of that year. The degree of direct state control over this sector has been greatly reduced since 1978, and growth in the gross value of agricultural output (GVAO) has been rapid 6.4% a year on average in 1980-89, although the rate moderated in the second half of the 1980's. In 1991 GVAO grew by 3.7%, down from 7.6% in 1990. To consolidate these gains and allow further productivity improvements. The strategy has been to divert peasant labour into the dynamic "township and village enterprises".

Even in the urban economy, the role played by state-owned enterprises (SOEs) is diminishing. In 1991 there were

104,700 SOEs producing 52.9% of industrial output, down from 54.6% in 1990 and 64.9% in 1995. Until recently, most of them worked to planned quotas, were subject to direct ministerial control and were dependent on the state for distribution of output and allocation of inputs, but control has to some extent been evolved to enterprise managers. The heavily loss-making state industrial sector was the main focus of the renewed drive for economic reform in 1992. New guidelines were published for the management of state-owned enterprises, giving them considerable autonomy, including in foreign trade.

Having achieved tremendous increase a agricultural output with its rural reforms, the government turned in 1984 to the more intractable problem of removing the obstacles to obtaining similar results in state-run industry. Its programme of urban reform had five main trends:

1. All urban enterprises would eventually be responsible for their own profits and losses and would operate in the market place, with capital to be provided by banks and inputs and output to be distributed commercially;
2. The government would gradually abandon its management control of most enterprises;
3. The principle "to each according to his work" was to govern pay, and workers were to be employed on fixed-term contracts;
4. Price subsidies would be abolished wherever possible and wages and prices allowed to find their own level; and
5. The collective and private economy was to be encouraged and state ownership would diminish.

The 1986-90 (seventh) and 1991-95 (eighth) Five Year Plans confirmed these goals, the achievement of which was termed "macroeconomic structural reform". Essentially, a three-tier economy was envisaged, composed of State-directed, collective and individual sectors, where the influence of the authorities would become more indirect as the size of the enterprise diminished. The most strategic area of industrial activity (including energy and transport) would remain state-directed, with the quota system and government control of their pricing broadly unchanged. Other forms of ownership and a much more market-oriented approach (whereby central directives were removed and decision-making responded to "macroeconomic levers") were to be encouraged across the spectrum elsewhere including agriculture. Nevertheless, the state would intervene where it is appropriate. The small scale collective or individually run sector, both urban and rural, would operate almost entirely outside the scope of state directives, with prices determined by supply and demand. In order to bring about this gradual transformation two areas of immediate action were identified. The first was a reform of the management system whereby the running of enterprises was to be freed from the control of party cadres and a professional managerial approach inculcated, including an emphasis on profitability. This can be seen in the introduction of taxation to replace the handing over of profits to the state by state-owned enterprises and in a determination to eliminate waste and reduce losses by penalties. Closure of persistently loss-making factories is now official policy. The second area of action involves the creation of a system of financial intermediation to act as the channel for investment and to operate on the basis of commercial criteria. The financial sector has been evolving rapidly. An example of this is the introduction of something approaching an interbank market in five cities. New techniques of economic management have tended to be tried out on an experimental basis in selected areas and then extended under the heading of "economic responsibility system", a term borrowed from the agricultural reforms. Such systems vary from place to place and according to the scale of enterprise. The new 1992 guidelines for state-owned industries were introduced gradually with, as in the past, the prestigious capital Iron and Steel works in Beijing selected as the high-profile guinea pig.

Planning in China

The economy is still, in theory, centrally planned with the five-year plans supplemented by annual targets against which performance is measured. The first Five Year Plan (1953-57), which followed the Soviet emphasis on building a heavy industrial base, was in general successfully carried through after three years of rehabilitation during which the government has restored output to Pre-war record levels, carried out land reform, brought inflation under control and established the framework for the nationalization of the economy. Industrial growth, in particular, was impressive, at 30% annually during the plan period, but agriculture was neglected. Agricultural output grew by only 4.5% per year and not all the increase was in food stuffs. Industry was making increasing calls on the agricultural sector for raw materials and, by 1957, agricultural production could not keep pace with these demands and feed a population growing at more than 2 % a year. The second plan, which started in 1958, fell victim to the Great Leap Forward, an attempt to industrialize and modernize China in one stroke. On the basis of fictitious statistics, fulfilment of final targets for many important industrial goods was claimed in the first two years of the plan but the natural disasters and the recession caused by the chaos and confusion of the Great Leap Forward upset the entire plan and it was abandoned by 1960. It was followed by three bad years of declining output, high unemployment and widespread famine. It was not until 1964 that industrial production was back at the 1957 level.

During the 1960s the broad lines of economic policy was based on giving the greatest weight to agriculture and light industry, partly at the expense of the heavy industrial sector. Although, there were some shifts in emphasis, the policy survived during and immediately after the Cultural Revolution. China embarked on progress, but order was restored by the second half of 1968. The industrial sector was most affected by the chaos, but soon recovered. The 4th plan, launched in 1971, was the most successful since the first, with sustained economic growth, particularly, in the industrial sector. It also marked a major change in emphasis towards borrowed technology and capital a move necessitated by China's economic backwardness and vulnerability following the abrupt withdrawal of Soviet aid in 1960, which left many vital industrial projects half completed.

The Fifth Five-Year Plan, which was due to have started in 1976, was delayed because of the internal political disruption following the death of Zhou Enlai and Mao. Then, at the fifth NPC in February 1978, the then party Chairman Hus Guofeng announced a comprehensive ten-year economic development plan (1976-85). This plan, which generally came to be called "four modernizations", was first outlined by Zhou Enlai at the fourth NPC in 1975 when he announced that China must commit itself to accomplishing "the comprehensive modernization of agriculture, industry, national defence and science and technology before the end of the century so that China's national economy will be advancing in the front ranks of the world."

But the ten-year plan, with its strong emphasis on heavy industry and imported technology proved to be too ambitious and was abandoned only one year after its launch. This was immediately followed by the introduction of a readjustment phase. The essential aim of which was to restore structural balance by cutting back capital intensive heavy industry and giving priority to labour-intensive heavy industry as a way of meeting domestic consumer demand and fueling China's export drive. Selective application of domestic resources and foreign exchange has construction materials. Another major goal was to invigorate the economy through management reform, enterprise reorganisation, a greater role for market forces and more emphasis on material incentives. The period of readjustment was to have lasted for three years, but was extended until the end of 1985. Meanwhile, the sixth Five Year Plan (1981-85) was published. It called for modest annual average rate of increase of gross social product (the gross value of the product of the agriculture, industry, construction and commerce sectors) of 4%, with agriculture and industry, each growing at that rate. Its publication was delayed until 1983, and it therefore had little influence on investment decisions and did not take account of the stimulus to output provided by reforms. The result was that growth accelerated each year. Both 1984 and 1985 were marked by particularly rapid expansion in output and excessive demand for investment, imports and consumer goods. Money incomes expanded far beyond the ability of the economy to satisfy demand and inflationary pressure built up.

The Seventh Five Year Plan (1986-90) took three years to draft, was accompanied by an unusual degree of debate and was completed early enough to affect the allocation of investment funds. It envisaged two years of consolidation, with output growth to slow and capital investment to be held back sharply. Investment priorities as in the previous plan, concentrated on easing bottlenecks in transport and energy. The emphasis continued on improved efficiency in the use of resources (energy consumption per unit of industrial output was to decrease by 2.4% a year) and on a more market oriented approach to output. The recommendations of the World Bank, that the broad goal of quadrupling 1980 output by the year 2000 could best be achieved by a relatively rapid expansion at the more labour and less resource intensive parts of industrial and service sector, were written into the plan. For the purpose of development priorities the country was divided into three zones. The eastern seaboard was to concentrate on the absorption of advanced technology and serve as the conduit for the introduction of new technology in general. The central region, where the majority of energy and mineral resources are concentrated, would give priority to their development. In the poorest western region, agriculture and animal husbandry were emphasised.

Under the Eighth Five Year Plan (1991-95), the growth rate of GNP was planned to average 6% per year as investment switched to agriculture, transport and communications. The service sector was targeted for rapid growth (from about 25% to 33 % of GVAO by the year 2000). Again, the first two years of the plan was envisaged as "consolidation", continuing the austerity programmes. However, in early 1992 Deng Xiao Ping intervened in economic planning by launching a campaign for"border reform" and more rapid growth. "Consolidation" was forgotton, as real GNP growth reached 12.8% in 1992 and 13.9% in the first half of 1993. Fears of overheating prompted another set of austerity measures in July-1993, which were largely abandoned at the Central Committee plenum in November.

At the 14th National People's Congress in 1992, the party committed itself to a "socialist market economy", a concept that was then enshrined in the country's constitution by the NPC of March 1993. The fundamental assumption is that the market mechanism is necessary for fast economic growth, and that central economic controls must be replaced by indirect "macro-economic" methods. Already, in 1988, the National

People's Congress had authorised the sale of land use rights, guaranteed the existence of private enterprises employing substantial numbers of workers, and separated management from government in state-owned enterprises.

The Indian Economy

The Indian economy has a strong element of duality. India is one of the ten industrialized countries in the world, with a high level of indigenous technological achievement extending into such fields as nuclear energy, space and satellite communications, oceanography, deep sea oil drilling and armaments manufacture. But three quarters of the population owe their livelihood to agriculture, which with forestry, mining and fisheries accounts for about a third of GDP. And, while there is a growing use of new agricultural technology - high yielding seeds and fertilizers on irrigated land, approximately two thirds of the cultivated land is devoted to rainfed agriculture dependent on the annual monsoon, and much of it for subsistence purposes. Until the 1980s, India was one of the slower growing developing countries. In the last decade, however, the pace has quickened. The Sixth Plan (1980/81 - 1984/ 85) achieved its average annual growth target of 5.4 per cent. The spread of the Green Revolution, both geographically and from wheat to rice, lay behind this acceleration. The industrial sector, however, performed below potential, mainly on account of infrastructure bottlenecks (power in particular) and a general failure to use physical and human capital productively. The Seventh Plan (1985/86-1989/90) achieved annual growth of over 5 per cent, although some weaknesses have become apparent, notably a growing balance of payments problem, as well as inefficiencies in industry and the slow diffusion of improved agricultural techniques.

The public sector has played a dominant role in India's

development though this operates primarily through controls rather than direct spending, which is comparatively modest. The public sector has played particularly prominent able in investment (40 per cent of gross capital formation in 1990/91). As part of process of economic reform. India's post-independence development pattern strong centralized planning, regulation and control of private enterprise, state ownership, trade protectionism and strict units on the penetration of foreign capital and technology is increasingly being called auto question. Although there are many political obstacles, the process gathered new momentum with the incoming Congress Government in 1991. The share of the public sector in GDP dropped from the 1 per cent to 26.4 per cent in 1990/91 in the first time for many years and is pecked to continue to fall with realisation.

Planning in India

Economic planning is far more important in India than in most non-communist countries. It provides the homework for determining public sector investment priorities and the rationale for roughly interventionist economic management. The First Plan, inaugurated in 1951, concentrated chiefly on agriculture and irrigation, while the Second (1956/57-1960/61) and Third (1961/62-1966/67) ran into difficulties because of suspension of aid and devaluation and was finally abandoned and restarted in 1969/70. The Fifth Plan gave equal weight to growth and distribution but it was rendered meaningless by the sharp deterioration in India's terms of trade, due particularly to increase in oil prices. The Sixth Plan (1979/80-1984/85) was intended to be more flexible, and was based on the principle of annual "rolling" plans. It set an average growth target for national income of 5.1 per cent and this growth objective was actually surpassed.

The Seventh Plan which had aimed at 5 per cent overall

growth also exceeded its target. The target was 4 per cent agricultural growth and 8 per cent growth for industry. While the aggregate growth figure was exceeded, however, agriculture and industry did not meet their targets and the high growth rate was explained by the rapidly expanding services sector.

The Seventh Plan envisaged a greater emphasis on the allocation of resources towards energy (mainly power development) and social spending at the expense of industry and agriculture, though, this did not happen.

There was much controversy about how the Seventh Plan was to be financed. The plan hinged on being able to raise public savings as a percentage of GDP from 2.8 percent during the sixth plan to 3.6 per cent during the seventh and being able to finance the growing claims of non-plan spending (on subsidies, defence and interest payments) from tax revenues. In practice this did not happen; public savings fell to an average 2.4 per cent of GDP during the seventh plan period, while foreign borrowing provided a substantially greater share of resources than expedited (1.9 per cent of GDP rather than 1.4 per cent).

The Seventh Plan entailed a total investment of Rs.3,224 billion of which 94 per cent was to be financed from domestic resources and 52 per cent from the private sector. Lying behind the investment assumption was a projected growth in the rate of gross investment from 19.6 per cent of GDP at the outset of the plan to 25.9 per cent at the end, and of gross savings from 18.2 per cent to 24.5 per cent. It was also assumed that through economic reforms it would be possible to achieve a much higher productivity of capital employed; it was hoped that the incremental capital output ratio (ICOR) for the Seventh Plan would be around 5, significantly better than in the Sixth Plan. In practice, not all these objectives have been realised.

The gross investment ratio averaged only 23.5 per cent and the savings ratio 20.2 per cent, both significantly down on the sixth plan. However, the ICOR was lower than expected, allowing India to get more output from less investment.

What now worries the planners most is that there has been a definite slackening in the momentum of savings and domestic investment. Domestic savings were about 10 per cent of GDP in the 1950s. The (gross) savings rate improved to almost 25 per cent in 1978/79 but has fallen back to around 20 per cent (though comparisons are difficult because of changes in the statistical series in 1980/81). Some of the factors that earlier encouraged savings, such as the spread of rural banking and the conversion of cash hoards into financial assets, have lost their dynamism. Critics of government policies have tended to focus attention on the spread of "luxury" consumption by the nouveau rich. A more measurable problem is the decline in public sector savings from a peak of 4.6 per cent of GDP in 1978/79 to 0.9 per cent in 1990/ 91, though the share of public sector investment in total investment has not declined. When savings are expressed in net rather than gross terms, the public sector's contribution becomes negative, dragging down the savings performance of the economy as a whole.

Gross capital formation as a percentage of GDP reached 23.3 per cent in 1978/79 and, having fallen slightly in the early 1980s, has retained a similar level in the last few years. Since the mid-1980s capital formation has exceeded savings by almost 2 per cent the gap being met by overseas savings (aid and credit). Nonetheless, with capital formation at this level, the poor returns from much investment (in electricity, for example) could be an explanatory factor. There is increasing concern with the poor performance of public sector enterprises in particular.

India and China—A Comparison of Their Planning Process

The schedule for the Eighth Plan has been badly disrupted by changes of government and by growing uncertainty over what role, if any, planning can usefully perform in a more liberalised economy. The plan was finally launched in April 1992 in a low key manner, with an emphasis on market-based policy reform rather than qualitative targets. However, the public sector still accounts for 45% of investment. The GDP growth rate was sought to be rated from 5% in the seventh plan to 5.0% in the Eighth Plan. To achieve this a substantial improvement was required in the areas of savings, investment, pattern of investment, growth on the export front, etc.

Conclusion

China's planned development may give India a lot of input for an improved development strategy. The management techniques followed by China have their own uniqueness. Like China, India is also combining the market economy with planned development although their patterns, ratios and objectives are different. It is now for India to gain from China's experience and follow its own priorities. Of course, one has to note that India and China are two different political systems and their economic development process cannot be diverted from this fact. However, it is not the similarity alone, but differences too offer important inputs for a developmental strategy.

REFERENCES

1. World Bank, *China—External Trade and Capital* (1988) Washington D.C., U.S.A.
2. Jagdish Bhagwati, *India in Transition: Freeing the Economy* (1993) Clarendon, Oxford.

3. C. Rangarajan, *Maximising Foreign Investment in Recent Development in India* (1993).
4. Sukumoy Chakravarty, *Development Planning: the Indian Experience* (1987): Oxford.
5. Robert P. Dernberger, "The Chinese Economy in the New Era" in *Chinese Economic Policy-Economic Reforms at Midstream*, Bruce L. Reynolds (ed) 1988.
6. Emmanuel C.Y. HSU, *The Rise of Modern China* (1990).
7. Gautam Mathur, *"Planning For Steady Growth"* (1965); Basil Blackwell, Oxford.
8. State Statistical Bureau; *China Statistical Year Book*, New China News Agency, (1990).
9. *India's Five Year Plan Documents*, Planning Commission, GOI.
10. Subramanian Swamy, *Economic Growth in China & India—1952-70-A Competitive Appraisal* UN: of Chicago Press (1973).
11. B. Satyanarayan, *India's Trade with Asia & The Far East Countries* (1986): B.R. Publishing Corpn, New Delhi.
12. B. Satyanarayan, (Ed) *A Comparative Study of Foreign Direct Investment in China & India* (1996), Himalaya Publishing House, Bombay.

2

Regional Disparities in Andhra Pradesh: Need for Balanced Development*

The problem of regional inequalities in development within nations (apart from between nations), is increasingly engaging the attention of social scientists all over the world. The issue assumes special significance in India, where the overwhelming majority live below poverty line. This is all more so because India's constitutional structure is somewhat federal in nature and considerable heterogeneity exists in terms of language and culture among the people of the different regions of India.

The main focus of Indian planning has been on economic growth with social justice. All along, our capital-centred and urban-oriented approach has been unable to make us neither self-sufficient nor solve the poverty and unemployment problems. Many people are of the view that inter-state and inter-regional disparities are a product of our planning process. The remedial problems could be the optimum utilisation of resources, dispersal of industries for balanced regional development and establishment of employment-oriented industries.

---

* Also appeared in S. Simhadri et al. (ed.) *Telengana: Dimensions of Underdevelopment*.

The degree of economic development of nation depends upon the integration and interrelation of industrial and agricultural sectors. Various studies point out that the modern industries, which have sprung up both at the national and regional levels, are not properly integrated and dovetailed into the rest of the national economy. Reports on industrialisation in independent India reveal that industrialisation is concentrated in and around established metropolitan and industrial centres. The most unhappy aspect of this kind of industrialisation has been the negligible share of the rural masses in the fruits of nearly five decades of industrial planning. This is particularly true of the backward region of Telengana, where the so-called modern industrialisation has centred around the twin cities of Hyderabad and Secunderabad to the great neglect of the remaining nine districts though the necessary resources exist there in plenty.

The NCAER report draws a similar conclusions. It states, "the state of Andhra Pradesh has not yet had a chance to develop as an integral economic unit". It came into being through the fusions of regions with diverse political backgrounds that had conditioned their economic discipline and background. Consequently, disparities exist not merely at the regional level, but also at other economically significant aspects of life, like habit patterns and social attitudes. Hence, the well recognised division of the state into three regions - Coastal Andhra, Rayalaseema and Telengana, though essentially political, has significant economic validity". Hence, the real integration of the state calls for a balanced growth by rectifying the regional imbalances among the three regions of the state.

Telengana region is endowed with rich resources like iron ore, coal, limestone, quartz, manganese, mica etc. They are either not yet tapped or are being excavated only is small quantities. If there could have been large scale industrialisation, which is not only agro-based, but also mineral and forest based, there could have been a higher rate of employment both or skilled and unskilled workers. Though the region is essentially agricultural in character, the pattern of industrial development even after 1956 does not indicate the utilisation of agricultural resources for industrial purposes to any significant extent as is evident from the fewer number of agro-based industries in the region.

In any strategy of development at the State level, one has to take note of the levels of development obtaining in the three regions of the State, viz., Coastal Andhra, Rayalaseema and Telengana. The three regions differ in their socio-economic conditions. The coastal area is largely dominated by the fertile delta, though it ends in the north in a predominantly tribal strip. The Rayalaseema region is chronically drought affected with limited potential for agricultural development. Telengana, though rich in mineral resources, has been lagging in economic development. Thus it is a fact that a major portion of the State is underdeveloped and the general image of Andhra Pradesh as being a prosperous state because of its rich coastal region is incorrect. The position of Andhra Pradesh is such that in the list of the more advanced states, it is likely to be at the top, thereby missing both the advantages.

Andhra Pradesh has 363 large and medium scale industries with a total capital investment of Rs.1,800 crores, employing 334900 workers. Likewise it has 31787 small scale units with a total investment of Rs. 397 crores employing 381, 000 workers (1977-'78). Nearly one-third of the small scale units arc reported to have been declared sick mainly due to the problems of working capital and marketing.

The regional distribution, district-wise and region-wise, of manufacturing activity in A.P. during the period 1977-78 showed that more than half the total output is in Coastal

Andhra (52.4), while it is 13 per cent in Rayalaseema and 34.6 per cent in Telengana. With the subtraction of Hyderabad, Telengana shows 10.6 per cent for the rural Telengana region. This is true for almost all the economic indicators.

TABLE 1

Regional Distribution of Manufacturing Activity (1977-78)

Sl. No.	District's	Factories (No.)	Productive Capital Per factory		Employment investment		Output Per factory	
			in Lakhs	in %	in Lakhs	in %	in Lakhs	in %
(a)	**Coastal Andhra**	3851	6.19	24.7	64	41.0	26.84	52.4
1.	Srikakulam	246	6.99	1.2	94	3.9	19.35	2.4
2.	Vishakapatnam	418	43.09	13.4	88	6.2	36.19	7.7
3.	E. Godavari	627	5.39	2.5	43	4.4	18.36	5.8
4.	W. Godavari	561	5.99	2.5	55	5.1	21.87	6.2
5.	Krishna	562	5.46	2.2	41	3.8	21.79	6.2
6.	Guntur	819	3.6	2.2	76	10.3	40.25	16.7
7.	Prakasham	419	1.51	0.4	91	6.8	30.56	6.5
8.	Nellore	199	2.37	0.3	60	0.5	8.47	0.9
9.	Kurnool	416	4.37	1.0	31	2.2	31.31	6.6
(b)	**Rayalaseema**	1088	4.05	3.3	32	5.7	23.69	13.0
10.	Anantapur	257	2.61	0.5	29	1.2	15.51	2.0
11.	Cudappah	167	6.24	0.8	29	0.8	19.14	1.6
12.	Chittor	248	3.69	0.7	37	1.5	22.45	2.8
	Telangana	3390	28.74	72.0	95	53.0	19.55	34.6
13.	Hyderabad	1061	79.14	63.0	111	19.8	44.27	24.0
14.	Medak	141	33.57	4.23	158	3.7	45.35	3.2
15.	Nizamabad	1015	2.20	0.80	114	19.2	5.05	2.6
16.	Mahabubnagar	252	1.34	0.3	9	0.4	2.17	0.3
17.	Khammam	75	6.69	0.4	45	0.6	13.32	0.5
18.	Warangal	157	3.93	0.5	67	1.7	11.85	0.9
19.	Karimnagar	402	4.01	1.2	70	4.7	3.75	0.7
20.	Nalgonda	122	1.69	0.2	25	0.5	14.07	0.9
21.	Adilabad	158	11.61	1.4	106	2.7	18.40	1.5
	A.P.	8329	16.12	100.00	72	100.00	23.10	100.0

Source: Report on Annual Survey of Industries, 1977-78.

Note: * - per factory investment in lakhs; **- % to State total.

Some broad indicators of development for the three regions are self-explanatory. Telengana compares well with the other regions; but with the exclusion of the metropolitan cities, the dismal reality is projected. If the number of tele-phone connections, of which 1,51,763 or 68 per cent are the twin cities alone.

TABLE 2

Selected Indicators of Development

Sl. No.	*Indicator*	*Coastal Andhra*	*Rayala-seema*	*Telen-gana*	*Total*
1.	Geographical Area (sq. Km.)	92.8	67.4	114.8	275.0
2.	% Area under forest	45.4	22.0	23.8	22.3
3.	Literacy (1991)				
	Male	55.69	58.57	52.95	55.13
	Female	36.10	30.68	29.21	32.72
	Total	46.22	44.96	41.29	44.09
4.	Population (1991/Crores)	2.87	.17	2.61	6.65
5.	Population Density	309	174	227	242
6.	Population Houseless (1991)	98021	4180	108665	250866
7.	No. Hospitals/dispensaries 1992-93 800	359	719	1878	
8.	No. of ploughs (1992-'93) in 000	842.3	620.5	1565.2	3028.9
9.	No. of tractors ('000)	27.8	10.5	17.9	56.3
10.	No. of Diesel Engines"	53.4	31.8	81.3	166.5
11.	PWD roads in Kms."	20.0	11.3	17.7	49.6
12.	ZPP & MPP roads in '000 Kms."	32.4	20.8	40.3	93.5
13.	No. transport/non-transport vehicles (31.3.93)	716.0	192.3	858.1	1766.4
14.	No. of post offices	6635.0	3705.0	5871.0	16211.0
15.	No. of Telegraph"	1881.0	992.0	1268.0	4141.0
16.	No. of Telephone connec.	174618.0	49731.0	222370.0*	446719.0

Source: Annual Report, Survey of Industries, 1977-78.

Note: * Hyderabad — 151763 connections, rest of Telengana = 70607.

The regional incomes, for the entire region and per capita, could be true indicators of economic growth, but these are not available. We always talk of transparency, objectivity etc., but when it comes to preparation of statistics on regional basis, it is deliberately sidelined and avoided. This being the state of affairs more often than not, we may not be able to argue on the basis of authenticity. This may be taken into consideration by the authorities that be, policy makers, leaders and the public in general. The statistics that are available for regional per capita income are confined to only 1961-1962. They are discontinued thereafter by the Directorate of Economics and Statistics, of A.P. The 1961-'62 figures however confirm the backwardness of Telengana in comparison to its other two counterparts.

TABLE 3

Indicators of Development–1961-1962

Sl. No.	*Indicator*	*Coastal Andhra*	*Rayala-seema*	*Telen-gana*	*Total*
1.	Per Capita income (in Rs.)	365	302	290	309
2.	Share of income from factory establishments in total regional income.	10.1%	2.4%	2.6%	3.7%

Some of the indicators bring out the facts as to how much leeway is still left for Telengana region, to make up and catch up with the relatively advanced and developed Coastal Andhra. The lines on which the development could take place are as follows:

(i) The state should provide more irrigation facilities by speeding up unfinished work on projects like Sriramsagar, Lower Manair, and start new projects at least at the rate of one big project per district and as many minor and medium irrigation projects as possible. Water conservation is of utmost importance. Even rivulets have to be tapped at various levels and water stored, so as to permit minimum evaporation. Whereever possibilities of lift irrigation exist, they should be encouraged. Other land reclamation projects ought to be carefully dovetailed into the overall rural development programmes, such as Protected Rural Works, Rural Housing Schemes, Primary Education and Health Scheme Centres, Roads and Rural Communications Schemes including market and feeder roads and rural electrification.

(ii) Production of agricultural implements, equipment, tools etc., should be speeded up. Other input-based industries such as organic and inorganic chemical industries and produce-based industries, such as alcohol from molasses, bakery products, cattle feed, condensed milk, vegetable and soap powder fruit and vegetables preservation, oilseeds crushing and refining, starches manufacture, etc. should be encouraged.

(iii) Large-scale and small scale industries that are resource based should be encouraged. Particularly, agriculture and agro-related industries display wide disparities (Table 4). The yields in the case of rice, ragi, bengal gram, red gram, groundnut, cotton, are very low while for the others they stand comparable. Since such inequalities reinforce the disparities, there is a need to frame well-targeted policies that may reduce such inequalities. The causes of low productivity need to be identified towards this end.

TABLE 4

Crop Yields*in Andhra Pradesh: 1992-1993

Sl. No.	*Indicator*	*Coastal Andhra*	*Rayala-seema*	*Telen-gana*	*State Average*
1.	Rice	2676	2211	2180	2495
2.	Jowar	720	1260	756	864
3.	Maize	2621	2420	2667	2260
4.	Ragi	1161	1164	851	1103
5.	Bengal Gram	740	549	312	469
6.	Red Gram	458	202	157	238
7.	Green Gram	451	543	426	436
8.	Black Gram	681	622	448	656
9.	Groundnut	224	733	866	828
10.	Sesame	258	272	218	242
11.	Castor	263	263	275	273
12.	Sugarcane	7272	7589	7004	7264
13.	Cotton	349	244	173	242
14.	Tobacco Virginia	1132	1134	1297	1152
15.	Others	2276	1155	1752	1870

As a first step toward planning in this direction - i.e. regional development, planning Boards at the State level (three regional Boards need to be set up), with planning cells at district level. A continuous flow of knowledge and information is to be ensured from the administrators in charge of district and block level planning are to be well informed and equipped with the requisite information (on knowledge and techniques of implementation); the local plans are to be oriented towards the resource base and fit into the broader framework of the regional plan. It is only then can one hope to achieve rapid growth with social justice for the region and the state as a whole.

REFERENCES

1. De Anil, 1968: *'Planned Industrialisation: An Approach to a Positive Strategy - Policy and Programme for India'*, Hyderabad.
2. Mathur, Gautam, 1969: 'Estimation of Telengana Development Fund', Memorandum submitted to the Govt. of A.P.
3. "_____", 1971: Keynote Address on the Framework of Regional Development', presented at the workshop on *Balanced Regional Development,* Dept. of Industries, Govt. of A.P., Hyderabad, Sept. 12-13.
4. "_____", 1972: 'Basic Choices in Development', *Indian and Foreign Review*, New Delhi, July 1.
5. Nadkarni, A.G., 1972: 'Development of Backward Areas', *The Economic Times,* Oct. 4 Government of Andhra Pradesh, 1972 *'Perspective Plan for Telengana - Resource Inventory'*, Planning and Cooperation Department, Vol.1.
6. National Council for Applied Economic Research (NCAER), 1962: Techno-Economic survey of Andhra Pradesh', New Delhi.
7. Satyanarayan, B., 1970: 'Development Potential of A.P., *Yojana,* May 17, 1973; Telengana Development, Problems and Possibilities',.*Indian Journal of Regional Science,* IIT, Kharagpur, Vol. V, No. 1.
8. "_____", 1984: 'Patterns and Possibilities of Industrial Development in India with Special Reference to A.P.', paper submitted at ULP Seminar organised at Satavahana Institute of P.G. Studies, Karimnagar, A.P., 26-27, March.
9. "_____", 1992: 'Process of Industrialisation in India - with reference to agro-industries in A.P.', paper presented at the Seminar on *The Industrial Policy and Growth of Agro-Industries in A.P.* organised under the auspices of Economic Committee, A.P. at Exhibition Grounds, Hyderabad, on 4th February.

3

Role of Multinational Corporations and India's Economic Development*

The first part of the paper is devoted to a discussion of the theoretical framework consisting of the principles of Development Economics suitable to a developing country like India with huge population background having necessary planning machinery. The second part deals with the role to be played by the Multinationals in achieving the goal of full-employment at the highest possible living standards attainable through the usage of the most modern mechanised techniques.

Theoretical Framework of Development Economics

At the outset, it should be made clear that any discussion relating to poverty, unemployment, inflation, etc., could be better understood in their proper perspective against the overall background of the national plan. As a matter of fact, it is the national plan which creates the disparities and imbalances and those could be effectively corrected only against the overall national background. The size of the plan should never be governed or limited by the financial resources that are available to the Government but is to be fixed only in terms of physical resources including the manpower skills

* Also appeared in VS Mahajan (ed.) Political Economy of Reforms and Liberalisation, 1997.

and the stocks of foreign exchange. Once the physical feasibility for the nation as a whole is established, the counterpart financial resources should be tapped either from the regular channels available to the Government or by resorting to the deficit financing, which of course, will have to be optimally allocated among various sectors so as to achieve a non-inflationary growth rate.

In modern growth theory of economics, the resources for development are physical resources which are the only bottlenecks on the path of development and not the financial resources. They are the natural endowments, the minerals and water resources, the qualities of soil, the productive capacity and stocks of each type of equipment and other inputs, the skilled manpower and foreign exchange, etc., and can be termed as the real resources and the shortage in any one of these can limit the plan size.

The proper criterion of measuring any country's backwardness is its per capita media income, rather than the average per capita income. The average per capita income is elusive in as much as it includes every one from the poorest fellow to the richest. A few millionaires can raise the per capita income figure while the total populace may remain in abject poverty.

It is certain that there has to be a long-term strategy for ensuring a continuous rate of growth. A choice has to be made between two fundamentally different types of strategies. In the first type, the consumption goods to be manufactured, are mostly the ones which are contained in a modern economy. If the planners choose to have this type for their economy, all these goods are either to be imported or manufactured within the country. The main idea in having this type of strategy is to start by providing all these items to the people at the top and then trying to spread their use downwards till the common man has got them. This is known as a Trickle-down theory. Our planning seems to be basically dependent upon this type of approach. But it has to be realised that the modern luxury goods produced with sophisticated technology take away a large chunk of national resources for their equipment which has to be necessarily of a high order of mechanisation and only a small percentage of the population can be provided with these goods. And this fraction of population happens to be not the lowest but the top stratum which keeps on getting promoted from Ice Boxes to Refrigerators and from there to the Deep Freezes, etc.[1]

When certain luxury goods are demanded by the consumers, it is forgotten that the particular demand does not represent the common man's demand of the country. When production is allowed to be geared according to the market demand, the planning process itself gets invalidated because planning should essentially involve common man's welfare. Normally, market demand flows from the amount of the wealth and income which people command at their disposal, rather than being decided by the planning process on the ground of the goods being essential for the people. In the former case, we cannot hope to achieve the pattern of development to lift up the masses of the region.

The alternative group of strategies aim at getting the necessities of consumption at a faster rate. They postulate a period of austerity in which only the barest minimum necessities of consumption per man will be manufactured but since the production will be carried out under a massive programme, the total product will be very high. The resources of the community are, therefore, spread more widely and evenly and do not cater only to the needs of a limited section of the population.

We can further divide the strategies pertaining to basic

necessities into two main types. In one of them, the necessities would be produced through the mechanised modes of production and in the other type through simple less mechanised techniques but improved implements.The mechanised prices of equipment require large inputs emanating from the Heavy-Investment Sector. They deplete the scarce resources of the Heavy Sector and prevents it from reproducing itself at a fast pace. The use of steel for basic industries builds the infrastructure for the future, while its use for the production of tractors or powerlooms helps to provide consumption goods for the present. There is thus, in this type of strategy, a direct conflict between the long-run and the short-run interest.

In the alternative development strategy the heavy investment sector does not divert its production to any substantial extent towards mechanised production in the consumption goods sector. Hence, the infrastructural base consisting of heavy engineering, steel mines, basic chemicals, fuel and power, machine tools, heavy transport, skilled manpower, etc., can grow very fast to make the country not only a modern one, but a self-sufficient one also, as regards the production of its key industries.

Under this strategy, the consumption necessities are produced by techniques which conserve the use of inputs from the scarce products of the Heavy Sector. These are cottage and miniature scale industries which save capital per unit of output to a very great extent. This strategy involves massive investment distributed over a large number of very small units in rural and urban growth centres[2]. On the other hand, widespread use of tractors and automatic looms reduces the rate of growth of employment both in the heavy sector and consumption sector. The use of either improved steel plough or power-tiller along with simple but improved implements provide not only widespread employment but a higher output yield per unit of capital invested. Consequently, it also provides consumption necessities to a large number of people.

The cost of mechanisation of consumer-oriented activities in a country would be to forego the alternative heavy investment projects whereas techniques which conserve the inputs of the heavy sector are only more employment creating but also permit more heavy investment to be undertaken. They give growth and social justice at the same time, whereas the tractor and the automatic loom hits social justice by lesser employment and hits economic growth through lesser possibility of production of heavy investment. Apart from this, the manufacture of highly mechanised equipment and their use also gives a high profit to wage ratio and unfavourable distribution of income which also creates the demand for luxury goods and a further distortion of the overall production as also its deviation away from basic necessities of an austerity economy.

It is therefore, no surprise that the strategy adopted by the Government both at the national and regional level, should have led to concentration of economic power and a very skewed distribution of income and wealth. The development strategy of a miniature scale industry and the improved plough or tiller technique provide for prosperity and a more favourable distribution of income and consumption apart from allowing heavy investment to grow fast.

Hence, the State has to decide on two basic issues. The first, whether it will continue the policy of producing luxury or semi-luxury commodities. To the extent they are produced, they should be totally exported to other countries so that precious foreign exchange could be earned. It should also be realised that in a relatively underdeveloped nation, luxury goods add more or less zero valuation to the national income since they do not add to the efficiency of the working population. On the other hand, it may create tensions and frustrations among the poorer sections of the population since it creates a sort of glass curtain economy.[3]

If the situation has to change, the basic level is to follow the austerity in the production and consumption of consumer goods by either cutting down or exporting all the luxury-oriented consumer goods and equipment to manufacture them. In many cases diversion to heavy investment is easily possible. The plastic material can easily be switched over from production of decorative laminates to low-friction gear boxes for vehicles.

The second decision to be made is regarding the technique of producing the essential consumer goods. One possibility is to undertake a widespread mechanisation both in industry and agriculture under the wrong assumption that they are more suitable and modern. This may be done under the delusion that the products produced through the mechanised techniques are cheaper. As a matter of fact, these products are exceedingly costly to the national economy in terms of economic priorities for building up the economic base in the long-run and producing social justice in the short-run.

The decision on two basic questions of choice of goods and choice of techniques must be made for National Planning. Only then the rest will follow. The long-term and short-term economic strength of a nation depends mainly upon the stock of heavy investment, capital and low-mechanised equipment for essential consumption goods, which it is able to accumulate in a balanced fashion over a given period of time. It is this factor which at the present as well as at a future date, will assure greater employment opportunities to all the eligible candidates. This in turn also ensures a standard of living for the median person to be somewhat above subsistence for the man at the top of the bottom quartile, which some people are enjoying in this country.[4] This should be the target of achievement in the shortest time and resources should be diverted from being used for giving a higher standard of living than this.

Role of MNCs in Developing Economies

This section is devoted to discuss the role of MNCs to be played in the overall developments of a developing country like India. Besides controlling the wage-rate developing countries cannot afford the parasitic consumption of luxuries. The luxury consumption should be effectively curbed through proper fiscal policy measures and a system has to be found out whereby the country exports all of these luxury items thereby importing the required heavy equipment. It is, of course, a matter of choice whether luxury goods are to be produced and exported or not to produce and neither export nor consume locally. Fortunately, the initial wage rate prevailing in the underdeveloped countries is generally low due to a subsistence wage rate.

When the population is growing at a high rate and the technology growing at a given rate, the importance of having a larger rate of growth of the economy than that of the growth of technical knowledge and growth of population need not be over-emphasised, as one has to catch up with back log of each one of these. Such a rate of growth can be had only in a Platinum Age.[5] Ultimately, a developing country such as India has to choose an optimum long-term strategy of development, which necessarily has to be based on a platinum age type of economic growth. An economy, to find itself on the path of steady growth, has to have all of its sectors growing at a uniform rate. There may be certain technical bottlenecks in some sectors. And it is these bottleneck goods which set the pace for the overall rate of growth. It is at this stage, the products of MNCs should solve the bottlenecks faced by countries such as India. Unless these bottlenecks are solved, the economy as a whole may experience only a slow rate of growth.

The limit to the size of a plan comes from the existence of certain bottleneck resources. These may be certain types of goods or skills, but they can never include money or finance for an efficient plan of development. When there is a vast amount of non-employment,[6] the planner can not solely rely on the investment to attain the goal of near full or full employment. The required savings could be augmented by the very means of investment. The planners should become aware that certain bottleneck goods exist which would be full employed at that size of the plan; and that these bottlenecks can not be removed by further investment in the short-run, and that no substitution of non-bottleneck goods for bottleneck goods is possible. The size of the plan is then a function of the set of the existing real goods, skills, foreign exchange, productive capacity, etc., and of the technology which can reproduce them or convert them into other goods. The products of MNCs which are sold in this country will have to be fitted into this overall framework of bottleneck commodities. The commodities other than bottlenecks should be banned. To the extent, MNCs are able to help developing nations like India to get over the hump of bottlenecks, they are welcome. Otherwise, they have no place in their economies. One can judge the efficiency of the method of planning which neglects the study of bottleneck real goods and pays attention mainly to the availability of financial resources as setting the limit to the size of the plan.[7]

It is a known fact that underdeveloped countries lack investible resources for their developmental projects, and usually turn for external assistance. Through MNCs, direct foreign investment of private entrepreneurs flows into the developing economy. Private entrepreneurs of MNCs, often generate new products and processes with new type of technical skills. These new processes if desired by the underdeveloped countries, could be transferred to the branch plants in a host nation where the needed product may be produced with the locally available resources. This may pave the way for technical diffusion. MNCs can also transfer their managerial and entrepreneurial skills to the personnel employed in host nations through their training centres. MNCs may also produce those goods, which otherwise a host nation may have to import from other external sources.

In other words, MNCs may produce the goods which are in the nature of import substitution.

Advocates of direct investment claim that MNCs help economic development in underdeveloped countries because foreign investors provide a package of capital, technology, management and organisational skill. In particular, they contend that foreign investors are able to mobilise both local and foreign capital that otherwise would not have been invested in the country. It is also argued that MNCs control within their organisations technology which developing countries cannot obtain from any other sources. Foreign investors are also able to provide uniquely qualified managerial personnel who are capable of providing training for both local labour and management personnel. The advocates of foreign direct investment feel that MNCs, with their worldwide production and marketing systems, are able to facilitate exports from developing countries. At the same time, their presence breaks down local monopolies and exposes local producers to rigorous competition, so that prices are lowered for consumers.

NOTES AND REFERENCES

1. Gautam Mathur, "Basic Choices in Development", *Indian and Foreign Review*, New Delhi, July 1, 1972.
2. Yadav Reddy, "Employment Creation & Growth", Presented at the Seminar on Growth Centres & Rural Development, held in Osmania University, Hyderabad, January, (1971).
3. Rasheed Talib, *A New Strategy for Growth*, Rachna Publications, New Delhi, (1972).
4. B. Satyanarayan, "Telangana Development Problems and Possibilities", *Indian Journal of Regional Science*, Vol. V, No. 2, (1973).
5. Platinum Age is that where (a) the level of wage is less than that of the Golden Age, and (b) the rate of growth is more than that of the Golden Age; it may be steady or unsteady. The rate of accumulation may be accelerating or decelerating. The main criterion is the least time span. For a detailed description of a Platinum Age see Gautam Mathur, "Investment Criteria in a Platinum Age", *Oxford Economic Papers*, (1967).
6. "Non-employment" refers to the case of underdeveloped countries where the workers were never previously employed in an organised advancing economy, whereas the term "unemployment" refers to people out of work who were previously employed.
7. One can compare India's Five Year Plans; Govt. of India, Planning Commission New Delhi.

4

Process of Industrialisation, Economic Reforms & Energy Planning in India*

A developing country like ours is still faced with quite a large section of population, which is not only illiterate and below poverty line, but also either unemployed or non-employed. The main focus of Indian Planning has been on growth and social justice. The mid-term appraisal of the Eighth Five Year Plan and the need to explore proper economic strategies for the ensuing Ninth Five Year Plan, has raised the question of recasting development strategies in right earnest. The capital-centred and urban-oriented approach has not been able to make India self-reliant or achieve removal of poverty or lessen unemployment and inequalities in the distribution of income to any significant measure all of which are the important objectives of Indian Planning.

The main reason as to why a large chunk of this country's population is still suffering from a sub-standard or sub-subsistence modicum of living is that no systematic thought has been given to provide the basic consumer's essentials to the target groups. It was expected that special employment and income generation measures would serve the purpose. Poverty was never considered as primarily remediable through

---

* Paper presented at seminar on Impact of Economic Reforms on S&T, 24-25 Feb. 1997.

systematic reduction of unemployment and under-employment. Hence, scarce resource which could have secured a continuing flow of employment and reduction of poverty in a systematic manner, have had to be diverted ' for the creation of adhoc opportunities of employment or poverty relief measures or welfare programmes. As a matter of fact the major flow in Indian Planning is that relevant production spectrum has never been designed on a long term basis to achieve consumer's equalitarianism through the choice of appropriate techniques, incomes and wages policies, employment and manpower planning. All these aspects of development strategies have been treated in isolation and not considered as a part of the total production and investment planning. The path chosen for economic developmentin India was neither exclusively capitalist in nature nor completely regimented one. As a matter of fact, a via media policy has been chosen which is known as the socialist pattern of society, wherein a compromise was made between the need to have an accelerated growth with social justice within the democratic framework. In a way, both the public and private sectors were called upon to play their respective roles.

Short-Run and Long-Term Growth

Whenever one talk of growth and development, it is meaningful to view the process of growth over a long period-All development efforts have to be geared to the long-term objective. What is created in the short-run should be viewed as an initial instalment of a long-term path of development. Whether it is growth, employment removal of poverty, all of them will have to be viewed as an essential part of the development process and a part of the overall plan. If one puts full employment as a short-term objective in a developing economy, it is as good as condemning it to perpetual underdevelopment. This could be achieved only by techniques of production which have a low productivity per man that even the payment of a subsistence level wage becomes unsustainable.

As opposed to this, if one goes in for a high degree of machanisation for the economy as a whole, it provides very little employment for the present as well as in the future because of the low rate of growth on account of the very high capital intensity per man. Under these circumstances, only the optimum technique is the proper vehicle for growth, employment and social justice, and it lies in between these two extremes. Here also, one has to make a distinction between the consumption goods sector and the heavy investment goods sector. The degree of mechanisation will have to be fairly low in the former sector when compared to the latter.

One school states that the short-term employment may be increased through production of goods which show a high demand potential.When we decide to allow production of goods on the basis of demand alone we come across goods which cater to the requirements of those who have high purchasing power. In the short-run, production of these goods may create more employment opportunities, but in the long-run it take's the economy away from the equalitarian structure (reducing disparities in consumption standard). It goes against the policy of social justice including the employment policy. Ultimately, it may bring about a regime in which goods percolate from the top towards the middle-income groups in a very slow fashion, while the common man's requirements are not fulfilled. Besides this it may also generate an economy in which modernised consumer durables are given substantial proportion of investment. Most of these goods could be produced only through highly mechanised form of production which offer very low employment per unit of capital investment. Thus, what is gained in terms of short-range employment through consumer luxuries is lost in terms of potentiality to give employment in the next period. This will lead to inter-gonerational gaps.

It may be emphasized that the short-run should not exist by itself but should be treated only as a segment of a longer horizon to which pertains a well thought out plan of development from the present conditions to the objectives to be attained in the long-term. It may be stressed that consumer necessaries could be produced by making use of the untapped resources, which in turn help the economy to expand the capital goods sector. Precious foreign exchange could also be earned by exporting some of these consumer goods produced by less mechanised techniques. At the end of the path of development the appropriate techniques may be different from the path and hence by the time we have finished traversing the path of development and enter the state of development all the population must be employed in the "golden age" technique.

Industrial Progress in India

The decade of 1980s witnessed, a rapid expansion of the industrial activity which can be attributed mainly to the reforms undertaken in both industrial and trade policies in the mid-eighties. Further policy change has become necessary for accelerating industrial growth and to control recession in the 1990s in order to consolidate the achievements of the last decade. The new policy initiatives are announced in the statement on industrial policy tabled in Parliament on 24th July 1991. The new package of industrial policy abandons industrial licensing in all industries except those reserved for public sector. Restrictions on investment by MRTP and FERA companies have also been removed. The MRTP Act has been amended to remove threshold limits of assets. Approval for foreign investment upto 51% of equity has been made automatic in specified high priority industries. An attempt is made in the present study to assess the performance of the industrial sector during 1971-1993.

TABLE 1

Annual Growth Rates of Industrial Production in India

Percentage change over previous year with 1980-81=100

Year	*Growth rate of industrial production*
1970-71	4.0
1971-72	5.7
1972-73	3.9
1973-74	0.8
1974-75	3.2
1975-76	7.2
1976-77	9.8
1977-78	3.3
1978-79	3.6
1979-80	-1.7
1980-81	4.0
1981-82	9.3
1982-83	3.2
1983-84	6.7
1984-85	8.6
1985-86	8.7
1986-87	9.1
1987-88	7.3
1988-89	8.7
1989-90	8.6
1990-91	8.5
1991-92	-0.1
1992-93	2.3
1993-94	6.0
1994-95	-8.6
1995-96	12.0

Compiled from different issues of "Economic Surveys" (Government of India).

The trends in the industrial growth during the study period could be seen from Table 1. It becomes evident from Table-1 that the industrial production has suddenly shown a negative rate of growth during 1991-92. In which year the new industrial policy was initiated. This is due to a severe recession. The trends relating to the post new industrial policy have shown some recovery. The industrial performance during 1992-93-94 is better than the earlier period. Of course the are well below the normal trend growth because of the then policies of import restriction, rise in the cost of imports due to the cash margin requirement and the downward adjustment of the exchange value of the rupee. The right money policy on the supply side and perceptible fall in effective demand due to inflationary pressure, reduction in public expenditure and strict fiscal discipline on the demand side have also caused the slow industrial growth. The annual growth during 1994-95 and 1995-96 is quite substantial.

Statistical information relating to the major sectors of industry during the pre and post liberalisation period are presented in Table 2. It may be noticed that from among, the different sectors of industry in the manufacturing sector which is major segment in Indian industrial production showed a decline in production of -0.8% in 1991-92 as against an average annual growth of 8.9% between 1985-86 and 1990-91. The mining sector grew by only 0,6% in 1991-92 while the electricity sector showed a growth rate of 8.5% over the previous year. These trends reveal that the impact of new industrial policy and liberalisation has not been uniform across different major sectors of Indian industry. Ofcourse, one finds that the growth rates have picked up in the subsequent years in almost all the sectors. One will observe that electricity generation has turned to maintain high growth rates throughout the period.

TABLE 2

Annual Growth Rates in Major Sectors of Industry

Year	*Mining (11.46)*	*Manufacturing (77.11)*	*Electiricity (11.43)*	*Percent General*
1981-82	17.7	7.9	10.2	9.3
1982-83	12.4	1.3	5.7	3.2
1983-84	11.8	5.7	7.6	6.7
1984-85	8.3	8.0	12.0	8.6
1985-86	4.1	9.7	3.5	8.7
1986-87	6.3	9.4	10.3	9.2
1987-88	3.8	7.9	7.6	7.3
1988-89	7.9	8.1	9.5	3.7
1989-90	5.3	7.6	10.8	8.6
1990-91	4.5	9.0	7.8	8.2
99=-91	0.6	-0.8	8.5	0.6
1992-93	0.6	2.2	5.0	2.3
1993-94	3.5	6.1	7.5	6.0
1994-95	6.2	9.0	8.5	8.6
April-Sept 1995-96	12.5	12.0	10.9	12.0

Source: Indian Economic Survey 1992-93 and 1995-96 (Government of India).

The programme of liberalisation and new industrial policy initiative aim at increasing the long term growth rate of GDP through deregulation, in both commodity and factor markets. In labour surplus economy like India these policy changes are likely to raise considerably and demand for relatively cheap unskilled labour since, much of the demand for labour is generated in non-farm sector, a shift in the employment structure is possible and is hopefully expected.

New Economic Policy and Its Impact on the Indian Economy

In 1991, a New Economic Policy was introduced with some measures. This policy was meant to resurrect the economy from the fiscal and balance of payments crisis. Sweeping market oriented reforms in industry, foreign trade and investment were introduced to liberalise the economy from various controls. The most serious problems facing the Indian Economy were as follows:

1. A large fiscal deficit was occuring;
2. A huge foreign debt with a high debt-service ratio and debt export ratio, which has recently caused a downgrading of the country's credit rating has led to serious repayment problems;
3. Low levels of efficiency in all sectors of the economy;
4. The recessionary situation in the industrial sector, stagnant agricultural output with poor growth prospects coupled with a high level of inflation;

The task before the government in June 1991 was two-fold:

(a) To restore economic stability by reducing fiscal and balance of payments deficit;

(b) to complete the process of economic reforms i.e., structural adjustments which have been contemplated for the last 10-15 years.

The salient features of the new economic policy are as follows:

1. The public sectors importance is gradually reduced and free market economy is favoured;
2. Towards this end, a policy of closing down

"Sick"public sector industrial units has been announced;

3. More free entry of the private sector in industries
4. Free entry to foreign capital and investments including foreign technology, transfers.
5. Freer imports following improvements in foreign exchange reserves situation.
6. No upper limit for monopoly business.
7. Opening of channels for utilising "black money" without asking any questions.

The New Industrial Policy has limited the scope of the public sector to only eight major acreas which involve infrastructure like Railways and strategic activities like exploration of minerals atomic energy and production of ornaments. The number of industries requiring licences has been reduced to only 18.

On the whole, impact of the new Economic Policy could be observed from two points of view.

Short-Term Measures

(i) Its impact on balance of payments crisis;

(ii) Repayment of external debt.

One could as well note that these problems have been solved to a very great extent because of the improvement in the international liquidity position.

Long-Term Measures

(i) The reviving of international credit-worthness;

(ii) How to control the price inflation;

(iii) How to reduce unemployment, poverty, illiteracy etc.

One is not sure that how far the new economic policy is able to solve these problems. Each one, requires a long-range planning with suitable monetary,' fiscal and physical instruments. But, on the other hand, New Economic Reforms imply liberalisation, which necessarily discard the significance of prioritisation.

Energy Planning and Development in India

Having discussed about the broad pattern of industrialisation which has taken place in this country, this section is devoted to discuss about the development of energy with all its related problems. India's energy requirements are considerable and growing. The country's per capita commercial energy consumption is less than a tenth of the world's average. Further, there is a great disparity between the urban areas and the rural areas. The urban areas consume 80% of the total energy use with only 30% population whereas the rural areas consumed only 20%. although they have 70% of the total population. An analysis of the major forms in which the energy is used in rural areas reveals that the share of non-commercial energy is 65%, of human and animal energy 15% and of commercial energy 20%.

The production of energy materials and power sector during the past four and half decades has grown or substantially. There is imperative need to develop and diffuse innovative renewable energy technologies besides To improve the efficiency of the conventional energy system several steps are to be taken. It is felt that the coal demand is likely to double over the next decade. By the end of the Ninth Five Year Plan the Coal demand is estimated to go up to 459 million tonnes from the present production of 228 million tonnes. Many energy scholars feel that during 6th and 7th Five Year Plans, a non-renewable energy resource like coal has been recklessly used by neglecting the inexhaustible energy source like water. The hydel-thermal energy ratio until the end of Fourth-Five Year Plan was 1.14, which is in the range of 1:2.5 at the beginning of Eighth Plan. It has, been estimated that more than 80% of the hydropotential still remains unharnessed despite the inherent advantages of irrigation, water shortage and flood control benefits of such schemes compared to thermal and nuclear schemes. Hence, a progmatic energy policy should lay stress on realigning the thermal hydro mix by undertaking more viable hydro-electric projects whereever it is feasible.

The Central Electricity Authority undertook renovation and modernisation of old thermal power plants during the Seventh Plan period. During the Eighth Plan period, the CEA plans to modernise 39 thermal plants at a cost of Rs 1123 crores. This step has yielded good results by increasing the peak load factor (PLF) from 44.3% at the beginning of the Sixth Plan to 56.5% during 1987-83.

It is opined that there is conservation potential of 25%, in the industrial sector. In the transport and agricultural sector the conservation potential is 20% and respectively. It, is estimated that nearly 80% of electricity is consumed in energy-intensive industries such as aluminium, iron and steel, textiles, fertilisers, cement, chemicals., paper etc. The consumption of electricity per unit of product is much higher than in developed countries. Conservation is possible in industrial as well as agricultural sectors. In India, transmission and distribution losses are about 21%, whereas in developed countries they vary between 6% and 12%, It is estimated that about 8 million tonnes of coal are wasted in India every year through wrong practices of storage, handling preparation and combustion of coal.

Solar energy, wind energy nuclear energy bio-energy, ocean energy are some of the new renewable energy options which have been experimented and commercialised by developing area-specific technologies. The vast potential of solar energy in India is being tapped through the thermal and photo voltaic source. Solar water heating systems have become very popular for industrial, commercial and domestic applications. A large number of hotels, dairies, textile mills, hospitals, vocational institutions have been using these solar heating systems. Wind energy is another renewable source of energy. Electricity from wind has become cost-competitive in many coastal locations of India. Wind energy potential is site-specific. Considerable technological development is required for large scale wind generation, Nuclear energy is less preferred due to nuclear radiation hazards associated with accidents in such plants apart from the cost factor. Attention is to be given for the development of bio-energy on a large scale. This type of energy is free from environmental pollution. It is based on locally available renewable sources such as trees and plants. Mini-Micro hydel projects are another source for power generation and it is estimated that India has a potential of over 5000 MW under this sector. This has been identified as another major thrust area for decentralised generation of, power during Eighth and Ninth Plan periods.

It is a fact that non-conventional energy in India has not yet become commercially viable. This is due to various reasons. Firstly, it is not dependable because most of the locations are very remote where maintenance standards of the technical systems are very poor. Secondly, this country has paid too much attention only to the conventional power sector. The non-conventional decentralised renewable energy development has not picked up till the -1970s. It is now a fully established fact that the decent: alised energy system has a significant untapped potential due to large bovine population, tropical climatic conditions and availability of a large number of wind power locations.

Analysis of World Bank's lending to various developing countries brings out the fact that preference was shown to the energy sector. South Asian and East Asian regions have received considerable quantum of foreign capital from the World Bank. It is also a fact that India is one of the major recipients of World Bank's lending to energy sector as far as developing countries are concerned. Similarly, India received substantial foreign capital from the Asian Bank. After the New Economic Reforms are introduced in 1991, there is good response for Foreign Direct Investment. A number of Multinationals are showing keen interest to invest in the energy sector. In view of this many experts feel that the government need not provide too many concessions for setting up power plants.

India can also seek international cooperation in the area of setting up of power links with neighbouring countries. For example, Nepal has shortage of capital but possesses enormous hydro potential. The power potential could perhaps be developed, if India is willing to invest and in turn draw substantial power generated for its own industries located in the proximity. Incidentally, these types of projects may prove beneficial to both the participating countries.

REFERENCES

1. Adelman, M.A., *The World Petroleum Market* (Bathemore; Johns Hopkins Press), 1972.
2. Asian Energy Problems: *An Asian Development Bank Survey*, Federal Publications, Singapore (1982).
3. Asian Development Bank, *Environmental Considerations in Energy Development* Manila (1991).
4. Bansal, N.K, Kishore, V.V.N. & Mishra, Anil (ed) *Energy Options for the 1990s*, Tata McGraw-Hill Publishing Co., New Delhi (1988).
5. Bhagwati & P. Desai, *Indian Planning for Industrialisation*, Oxford University Press (London), 1970.

6. Balasubramanyam, V.N. *International Transfer of Technology to India*, New York-Praeger (1973).
7. Pachauri, R.K. *Energy Policy for India*, New Delhi 1980.
8. Pachauri, R.K, *Energy India Studies*, Macmillan, 1976.
9. Parik, Kirit, *'Energy India Studies'*, Macmillan, 1976.
10. Mahajan, V.S. (Ed) *'Studies in Energy and Economic Development'* Deep & Deep, New Delhi, 1991.
11. Sharma, L.C. & Mehta, R., *Economic Development and Non-commercial Energy in India*, 1988.
12. World Bank, *Energy in Developing Countries*, 1980.
13. Schumacher, E.F. *'Small is Beautiful'*, Blond 'Briggs Ltd., London, 1973.
14. Bettlehem, *Studies in the Theory of Planning*, 1959.
15. Lewis, Arthur, W, *Development Planning the Essentials of Economic Planning* (1966).
16. Robinson, Joan, *Essays in the Theory of Economic Growth*, 1964.
17. Rostow, W.W, Economics of Take-off Into Self-sustained Growth' 1964.
18 Nurkse, Ragnar, *Problems of Capital Formation in Underdeveloped Countries*, 1966.
19. Myint, H *'The Economics of the Developing Countries'*, 1965.
20. Mathur, Gautam, *'Planning for Steady Growth'*, Basil Blackwell Oxford, 1965.
21. Mathur, Gautam, 'Disparity Tax a compsite Economic' 1975.
22. Satyanarayan, B, *'India's Trade with Asia and the Far East Countries' with special Reference to Trade Policy for a long-term strategy of Development,'* B.R. Publishing Corpn. New Delhi, 1986.
23. Satyanarayan, B. (ed) *'A Comparative Study of Foreign Direct Investment in China & India-Problems & Perspectives'* Himalaya Publishing House, Bombay, 1996.
24. Satyanarayan, B.(Ed.), *Social Sciences & Planning for Sustainable Development'*. Himalaya Publishing House, Bombay, 1977.

5

Trends in India's Economic Growth Since Independence*

A developing country like India is still faced with quite a large section of population, which is not only illiterate and below poverty line, but also either unemployed, underemployed or non-employed. The main focus of Indian Planning has been on growth and Social Justice. The mid-term appraisal of the Eighth Five Year Plan and the need to explore proper economic strategies for the ensuing Ninth Five Year Plan has raised the question of recasting development strategies in right earnest. The capital-centred and Urban-Oriented approach has not been able to make India self-reliant or achieve removal of poverty or lessen unemployment and inequalities in the distribution of income to any significant measure all of which are the important objectives of Indian Planning.

The main reason "as to why a large chunk of this country's population is still suffering from a sub-standard or sub-subsistence modicum of living is that no systematic thought has been given to provide the basic consumer's essentials to the target groups. It was expected that special employment

* Paper presented at National Seminar on Fifty Years of Development Experience, Aug. 1997, Mysore.

and income generation measures would serve the purpose. Poverty was never considered as primarily remediable through systematic reduction of unemployment and under-employment. Hence, scarce resources which could have been utilised for creating assets, which in turn could have secured a continuing flow of employment and reduction of poverty in a systematic manner, have had to be diverted for the creation of ad hoc opportunities of employment or poverty relief measures or welfare programmes. As a matter of fact the major flaw in 'Indian Planning is that a relevant production spectrum has never been designed on a long term basis to achieve consumer's equalitarianism through the choice of appropriate techniques, incomes and wages policies, employment and manpower planning. All these aspects of development strategies have been treated in isolation and not considered as a part of the total production and investment planning. The path chosen for economic development in India was neither exclusively capitalist in nature nor completely a regimented one. As a matter of fact, a via media policy has been chosen which is known as the socialist pattern of society, wherein a compromise was made between the need to have an accelerated growth with social justice within the democratic framework. In a way both the public and private sectors were called upon to play their respective roles.

In this paper an attempt is made to study the performance of GDP growth of India for two periods one before eighties and the other after that. This is because since 1980s the country has witnessed a major change in its industry, trade and development policies, moving essentially from a closed import-substitution phase to a liberalised export-oriented market phase. Here it is also seen that growth performance of GDP is meaningful only if its relevance to stability, spatial distribution, its self-sustainability and welfare components are also analysed side by side.

There is a general feeling that it is only the tertiary sector and especially the value-added generated in defence and public administration which are the main contributing factors explaining this apparent acceleration in India's growth process. Of course, they cannot be isolated from the nature of the growth vis-a-vis their sustainability, stability, spatial distribution among the different classes of society. This is because it is well accepted that India has absorbed, in a comparatively better way, some of the external shocks from abroad such as bad monsoons by isolating her growth process from these shocks.

The slow growth of the Indian economy upto the late 1970s has been a cause for concern. The trend rate of growth of GDP appeared to have stabilised at 3.5% per annum. This was considered low especially when the average rate of growth in other developing countries was around 6% upto the mid-seventies. Shetty's study (1978) of economic growth in India since the mid-Sixties showed an improvement in the growth of the primary sector, especially in agriculture, but a drastic slow-down in the manufacturing sector.

In agriculture, although the Green Revolution had brought about an increase in overall output, the increase in the rate of growth had not been impressive, as the impact of the new agricultural strategy remained confined to the north-west and some parts of South India. Between 1967-68 and 1974-75, with growth in wheat production of 5.4% per year, rice production increased only at about 1.2% per year.

The performance of the secondary sector, particularly organised manufacturing industry was more dismal. There was a marked deceleration in the growth rate in the industrial seetor after the mid-1960s. This was a contrast to the industrial performance of the first Three Plans. The rate of growth for the peciod 1965 to 1976 was 4.1% compared to the growth rate of 7.2% during 1955 to 1960 and 9% during 1960 to 1965 (Shetty, 1978).

TABLE L

India's Growth Rate of Real GDP and its Main Sectors

Period	*Primary*	*Secondary*	*Tertiary*	*GDP*
1. 1951-52/1959-60	2.7	6.0	4.0	3.6
2. 1960-61/1969-70	1.6	5.3	4.3	3.2
3. 1970-71/1979-80	1.8	4.6	4.5	3.4
4. 1980-81/1990-91	2.1	6.9	6.3	1.9
5. 1991-1992/ 1996-97	3.6	8.1	7.3	6.5

Source: 1. Nagraj *Eco. & Political Weekly*, June 30, 1990.
2. *Economic Survey*, GOI, 1996-97.

Several studies have been made to look at the performance of the Indian economy since 1950s. It may be seen from the above mentioned table that there has been a marginal increase in agricultural growth in the 1980s in relation to the previous two decades. Thus, while the tertiary sector has witnessed a steady increase in growth over the successive decades, in 1980s the Secondary sector has shown the fastest rate of growth. Growth in the sub-sector manufacturing at 8.2% has been significantly higher than the rate of growth of 4.9% in the 1970s. During 1990s, the growth rates have been very buoyant.

Joshi and Bhargava attempted to locate the source of growth i.e., whether the growth arises in the public sector or in the private sector. If the sample period is divided as 1975-76, then most of the increase in GDP growth arises in the private sector.

If the sample is split at 1980-81, then the performance of the private sector is even better. Manufacturing in the private sector shows an increase from 4.14% to 7.69%, transport, storage and communication from 5.51% to 9.83%. All these details are shown in Table 2.

TABLE 2

India's Growth Rates by Industry

Sl. No.	*Sector/Item*	*1960-61 to 1980-81*	*1980-81 to 1989-90*	*1992-97*
1	2	3	4	5
I.	Agriculture and Allied Sectors	2.21	2.27	3.6
II.	Industry:			
	Mining, Manufacturing, Quarrying, Construction, Electricity etc.	4.38	7.87	8.1
III.	Services:			
	Trade, hotels, transport and Communication, Financing, Insurance, Community	4.25	5.25	7.3
IV.	GDP at Factor Cost	3.37	5.01	7.0

Source: Bhargava S & V Joshi; *Eco.& Political Weekly* Dec: 1-3, 1990; and *Economic Survey 1996-97;* GOI, Planning Commission.

If a long-term view is taken then it is the performance of the tertiary sector that is important. The decline in the share of the prirnary sector in Net Domestic Product frorn 58% in 1950-51 to 35 in 1986-87 has been matched by a rise in the share of the secondary sector from 15.1% in 1950-5l to 26.5% 1986-87 and a rise in the share of tertiary sector from 15.1% in 1950-51 to38.8% in 1986-87.

Bhattacharya and Mitra (1990) have characterised this as the "excess growth of the tertiary sector". This has been used to explain the divergence between agricultural and industrial growth rates. The sectoral distribution of Net Domestic Product are recorded in Table 3.

Bhattacharya and Mitra argue that high growth in the tertiary sector has been associated with a higher growth in income in relation to the growth in employment. According to them, this has led to a higher demand for industrial products

TABLE 3

Sectoral Distribution of Net Domestic Product (1980-81 Prices)

(percent)

S.No.	*Sector*	*1950-51*	*1960-61*	*1970-71*	*1980-81*	*1986-87*
1.	Primary	58.26	53.94	47.78	41.22	35.14
2.	Secondary	15.13	18.16	21.26	22.47	26.48
3.	Trade, hotels	8.84	10.18	11.49	13.00	13.34
4.	Transport	1.80	2.17	2.34	3.38	4.10
5.	Storage etc	7.32	7.12	7.33	8.46	9.25
6.	Community Services (including -PAD)	8.64	8 .42	9.90	10.97	11.94

Source: Bhattacharya & Mitra, *Eco & Political Weekly*, Nov. 2, 1990.

compared to the demand for agricultural products which in turn has resulted in disparities in the 'growth rates of two sectors. They also proceed to argue that, higher growth rates of services sector in comparison with the commodity sector is likely to result in either inflation or higher imports with an adverse effect on the balance of trade. This has the presumption that the services sector has a lower savings propensity than the national average. Dr. Gupta (1989) has demonstrated by cross country analysis of more than (150) countries that the saving propensity can be seen to go down whenever the services sector component of GDP in a Country rises.

Growth of the tertiary sector in India explains that there has been an increase in the share of this sector in national product. Table 3 shows the changes in the composition of the net domestic product since 1950-51. One may notice the importance of both the Secondary and tertiary sectors through time.

It is a feature common to many macro-economic theories that an increase in output, may be purchasable by a combination of higher inflation with redistribution of income and current account deficit. This is the case in the Structuralist models of inflation (Cardoso,1981) which argue that with a food supply constraint, a higher output in the non-food sector can be obtained by squeezing wages via inflation. Of course, if imports are possible, the supply constraint will be eased. This will be reflected in the balance of payments rather than in inflation. If higher output levels are associated with greater investment, the process will result in faster growth. In the context of this framework, we may consider the relative inflation and the current account performance of the 1980s in comparison with the earlier period. The following table records the figures relating to the rate of inflation measured by the consumer price index for industrial workers.

TABLE 4

Annual Rate of Inflation in India

1960-70	6.4%
1970-80	8.0%
1980-90	9.5%
1990-95	9.1%
1995-96	7.6%
1996-97 (Jan. 11)	5.7%

Source: Economic Surveys.

Inflation in the eighties and nineties is relatively higher when compared to the previous decade. This is inspite of the fact that 1970s witnessed two major oil price shocks.

The balance of payments situation has worsened significantly in the 1980s. A comparison of the current account balance of the 1970s, 1980s and 1990s is of interest. The following table records figures relating to the balance of payments.

TABLE 5

India's Balance of Payments (Us $ Million)

Year/Period	*Currenct Account Deficit*
Average- 1970-80	637
Average- 1980-87	3,418
1980-81	2,095
1981-82	3,149
1982-83	2,841
1983-84	2,3,99
1985-86	4,844
1986-87	4,562
1987-88	4,853
1938-89	7,996
1989-90	6,837
1990-91	9,680
1991-92	1,178
1992-93 (P)	3,526
1993-94 (P)	1,158
1994-95 (QE)	2,634
1995-96 (Q.E)	5,434

Source: Economic Surveys; GOI (Various issues).

Note: (P) Preliminary Actuals.
(Q.E) Quick Estimates.

It may be observed from the foregoing table that the deterioration in the external situation has continuously shown a consistently rising tendency during 1980s. The trade deficit as well as the deficit on the current account have increased substantially although the latter decade did not witness external shocks, equivalent to the oil price increases of the 1970s. It may be observed that the deficit has started declining from 1991-92 onwards and it is barely of the order of only $ 315 million in 1993-94. The current account deficit as a proportion of GDP has more than doubled in the 1980s, to 2.7% by 1987. As a consequence, India's external indebtedness has risen to more than $ 80 billion, according to the world Bank estimates. Measures to meet, the external imbalance will have to be taken soon, and this is likely to include some measure of discipline like reduction with regard to the fiscal deficit. In addition, some of the switching policies which are likely to be introduced, such as restrictions upon imports, may also lower future growth prospects. In short, there is some doubt whether the higher GDP growth of the 1980s is likely to continue into the 1990s.

REFERENCES

1. Todaro, Micheal P. *Economics For a Developing World,* Longman Group Limited; London (1979).
2. Hirschman, Albert O. *National Power and the Structure of Foreign Trade,* University of California Press, Berkeley (1945).
3. Myrdal, Gunnar, *Asian Drama,* Vol I, Penguin Books (1968).
4. Bairoch, Paul, *The Economic Development of the Third World Since 1960,* Methuen & Co. Ltd. London (1975).
5. Vora, DC, *India's Aid Diplomacy in the Third World,* Vikas Publishing House, New Delhi, (1980).
6. Gupta S.P., *Planning and Development in India: A Critique,* Allied Publishers, New Delhi (1989).
7. World Bank, *World Development Report,* Washington DC, (1989).
8. Sen, A.K., *Poverty and Famines: An Essay, on Entitlement and Deprivation*: Oxford; Clarendon Press (1981).
9. Chakravarty, S., *Development Planning: The Indian Experience,* Clarendon Press, Oxford (1987).
10. Bhagwati, J.N; and Desai, P. India: *Planning for Industrialisation,* Oxford University Press, London (1970).
11. Satyanarayan, B. "India's Industrial Progress in the context of New Economic Policy and Liberalisation"; in K.R. Gupta (Edited)

Liberalisation and Globalisation of Indian Economy, Atlantic Publishers, New Delhi (1995).

12. Tarlok Singh, *Poverty and Social Change,* Orient Longmans, New Delhi (1969).
13. Arthur N, Lewis, *Development Planning—The Essentials of Economic Planning,* (1966).
14. Ragnar Nurkse, *Problems of Capital Formation in Underdeveloped Countries,* (1953).
15. Joan Robinson, *Accumulation of Capital* (1953).
16. Gautam Mathur, *Planning for Steady Growth* (1965).
17. -do- *Disparity Tax in a Composite Economy* (1975).
18. B. Satyanarayan, *India's Trade with Asian and the Far East Countries (with Special Reference to Trade Policy for a Long-Term Strategy of Development,* B.R. Publishing Corporation, New Delhi (1986).
19. -do- (Edited), *A Comparative Study of Foreign Direct Investment in China and India- Problem and Perspective.* Himalaya Publishing House (1996).
20. -do- (Edited), *Social Sciences and Planning for Sustainable Development,* Himalaya Publishing House, (1997).

6

Inter-State and Inter-Regional Disparities in India and Sustainable Development

The problem of regional inequalities in development within nations (apart from between nations) is increasingly engaging the attention of social scientists all over the world. The issue assumes special significance in India where the ever whelming majority of the people live below the poverty line. This is all the more so because India's Constitutional structure is somewhat federal in nature and considerable heterogeneity exists in terms of language and culture among the people of the different regions of India.

The main focus of Indian Planning has been on economic growth with social justice. All along, our capital centred and urban-oriented approach has not been able to make us either self-reliant or it could solve the main problems of poverty and unemployment. Many a people are of the view that inter-state and inter-regional disparities are a product of our planning process. The remedial problems could be the optimum utilisation of available natural resources, dispersal of industries for balanced regional development and establishment of employment oriented industries.

The degree of economic development of a nation-region depends upon the integration and inter-relationship of industrial and agricultural sectors. Various studies point out that the modern industries which have sprung up both at the national and regional level are not properly integrated and dovetailed with the rest of the economy. Reports about industrialisation in Independent India say that the industrialisation is concentrated in and around established metropolitan and industrial centres. The most unhappy aspect of this kind industrialisation has been the negligible share of the rural masses in the fruits of nearly five decades of Industrial Planning.

Regional Disparities in India

Regional disparities exist in all developed and under developed countries of the world. The task of regional planning in UDCs is far more complex. Because of widespread poverty and below-subsistence level of existence of the vast majority of people in many backward regions of these countries, the task of two-fold.

(i) Reduction of regional disparities;

(ii) Ensuring atleast a minimum level of subsistence to the majority of people inhabiting the backward areas and living below the level of subsistence.

The strategy of deliberate promotion of "Growth Centres" can go a long way in accomplishing the former. Table 1 gives estimates of per capita income for different states of India at current prices.

TABEL 1

Per Capita State Net Domestic Product in (15) Major States (At Current Prices) in Rupees

Sl.No.	*State*	*1960-61*	*1980-81*	*1992-93*
1.	Andhra Pradesh	314	1380	5802
2.	Assam	349	1200	5056
3.	Bihar	216	868	3280
4.	Gujarat	380	1951	7586
5.	Haryana	359	2370	9609
6.	Karnataka	292	1623	6313
7.	Kerala	278	1513	5065
8.	Madhya Pradesh	274	1183	4725
9.	Maharastra	419	2427	9270
10.	Orissa	226	1231	3963
11.	Punjab	383	2690	10857
12.	Rajashan	271	1222	5035
13.	Tamilnadu	344	1498	6205
14.	Uttar Pradesh	244	1278	4280
15.	West Bengal	386	1580	5901
	Average	305	1630	6929

Source: "Indian Economy (1995) Misra & Puri.

Disparities in Industrial Growth

The initial distribution of industries was determined by the historical processes of growth reflected in the interests of the British Rulers. As a result, most of the industries got concentrated at a few centres. This pattern continued in the post-Independence period as well. For instance, a study of (28) large-scale industries in 1950 showed the dominance of the Western region, while 25% was concentrated in Western region, West Bengal accounted for 63% of total persons employed, 60.5% of gross ex-factory value of output, and 64% of Value added by manufacture.

This pattern of concentration has not changed substantially during the planning period despite all attempts made at regional dispersal of industries. For instance, as late as 1989-90, two states, namely; Maharashtra and Tamil Nadu accounted for 27.3% of factory empoyment, 26% of fixed capital, 32% of gross output, and 35% of value added by manufacture.

Disparities in Agricultural Development

Regional disparities have increased over time with the States of Punjab, Haryana, parts of Uttar Pradesh pushing well ahead of others. This is due to the HYV etc. For example, in 1990-91, per capita output of foodgrains, was 968 Kgs. in Punjab which was (5) times the national per capita output (197 Kgs).

Other Indicators of Disparities

(a) Urban population;

(b) Domestic Electricity consumption per capita;

(c) Road length per 100 km. of area;

(d) Percentage of villages connected with all-weather roads;

(e) Per capita bank deposit;

(f) Infant mortality rate;

(g) Literacy rate;

(h) Population below poverty line.

Population Below Poverty Line

Table 2 shows the population below the poverty line in various states in India.

TABLE 2

Population Below Poverty Line in Various States

Sl.No.	*State*	*1983-84*
1.	Bihar	49.5%
2.	Madhya Pradesh	46.2%
3.	Uttar Pradesh	45.3%
4.	Orissa	82.8%
5.	Tamilnadu	39.6%
6.	West Bengal	39.2%
7.	Andhra Pradesh	36.4%
8.	Karnataka	35.0%
9.	Maharashtra	34.9%
10.	Rajasthan	34.3%
11.	Kerala	26.8%
12.	Gujarat	24.3%
13.	Assam	23.5%
14.	Haryana	15.6%
15.	Punjab	13.8%

Source: CMIE, Sept. 1988 & 1994.

As far as poverty is concerned, in 1983-84 the proportion of the poor was the highest in Bihar (49.5%) and the lowest in Punjab (13.8%). May be, this is due to the higher level of per capita and percentage of irrigation in Punjab. Inversely, Bihar has the lowest per capita income while Punjab has the highest.

So far as Kerala is concerned, the poverty ratio has declined from 47% in 1977-78 to 26.8% in 1983-84. People attribute this steepfall to three reasons:

(i) Due to remittances from migrants to the Middle East Countries;

(ii) Due to the extensive Welfare Programmes; and

(iii) Due to relatively lower population growth.

Likewise, Assam seems to have recorded a noticeable fall in the proportion of population below the poverty line. On the other hand, Punjab has the lowest poverty ratio and is not particularly known for having adopted by any welfare programmes as is done in Kerala and some other states. But Punjab has consciously or unconsciously set to provide a firm production base which has helped to maintain the lowest poverty ratio. If this is so, it holds a lesson to others.

Given the socio-economic structure, the decline in the poverty ratio is generally the result of growth achieved, especially in agriculture and the effective implementation of various poverty alleviation programmes like NREP, RLEGP, JRY etc. These anti-poverty programmes have to be area and community specific, in order that their benefits may be wide-spread. They have to offset the uneven effects of economic progress on the poorer sections in different areas. Generally, the tendency is to select the easily accessible areas and politically dominant groups. The numerical targets may thus be attained but the basic purpose of the programme will not be served. Planning at the block, district and region within the State level has been devised to counteract this tendency.

It is very often expected that the fruits of "development" will percolate to the weaker sections of the society. It is a fact that in India the poverty ratio has no direct relationship with the existing per capita income level. While per capita income is rising, poverty ratio is more or less constant. It is time that the overall economic, agricultural, industrial and technological development is a condition necessary but not sufficient to eradicate poverty and undernutrition. There is a reason to believe that the very momentum of the developmental process has served to accentuate socio-economic disparities. Therefore, the challenge of development, for countries like India, which have chosen democratic political system, lies in devising ways and means of ensuring equitable distribution of the benefits of economic growth not only among various sections of population but also in various states and regions across the country. Only then the development could be properly sustained.

Data from country-wide diet surveys carried out by the National Nutrition Monitoring Bureau (BNMB) shows that diet in more than half of the households surveyed in Kerala are inadequate, while the percentage of these households is in the range of 40% in Andhra Pradesh and Orissa. The position of Karnataka looks far better, in the sense, that only 13% of the surveyed households are suffering from inadequate diets. Table 3 shows the proportion of households with inadequate calorie intake.

TABLE 3

Distribution of Households According to Dieting Inadequacy

Sl. No.	*State*	*% of HHS with inadequate Diets in Calorie and Proteins*
1.	Punjab	N.A.
2.	Kerala	53%
3.	Maharashtra	N.A.
4.	Andhra Pradesh	38%
5.	Orissa	42%
6.	West Bengal	29%
7.	Karnataka	13%

Source: "EPW", Dated 17-12-1983.

All these exercises boil down to one important point. If the pace of development in most of the States which are below the All-India Average Per Capita State Income is not accelerated, there is every possibility of their sliding down still further. Thereby, the sustainability of a balanced development in the country as a whole become very difficult.

This process could be combated to a very great extent by means of effective industrialisation. Some broad policy issues are:

1. Optimum utilisation of natural resources with emphasis on conversion of raw-materials into value-added products within the State.
2. Dispersal of industries to get balanced regional development.
3. Encouraging employment - oriented industries.

Policy of Sustainable Developmcnt

The move towards liberalised economic policies in the recent past arising out of the logic of competition has led (given the pattern of income distribution in the context of a mixed economy), to profit-seeking investment in consumer's durables and luxury consumables demanded by the upper and middle income groups. It has resulted in the import of recitative technology and adverse balance of payments including an abnormal increase in external debt. The liberalisation policies are encouraging capital and energy intensive techniques leading to depletion of natural resources and degradation of environments.

Environmentalists fear that the thrust of the New Economic Policy will result in greater pollution as the authorities will be tempted to be lenient towards industries in the interest of economic growth. They also apprehend that given the lax implementation of environmental laws, this country may attract "dirty" industries from the West. Added to this, growth of consumerism, particularly in urban areas, will lead to a spurt to urban pollution, unless higher pollution control standards are introduced and implemented strictly. On the other hand, industrialists fear that if environmental laws are made too strict, investment in the country including foreign investment may decline. They argue that voluntary environmental audits will be better that statutory ones, as the latter may bring about a mere mechanical compliance. They want pollution control standards established through a dialogue between the industry and the government, rather than unilaterally. It is clear that environmental protection cannot be looked upon as an after thought. It needs to be integrated into planning and costing of all industries. Once, this is accepted, the change in economic policies need not spell environmental disaster, thereby paving the way for a better development sustainability.

REFERENCES

1. Michael, P. Thodaro, *Economic Development in the Third World*: Longman, New York, (1981).
2. Gunnar Myrdal, *The Challenge of World Poverty*, New York, Pantheon (1970).
3. Hollis B, Chenery, (Ed) *Studies in Development Planning*, Cambridge, Mass, Harvard University Press (1971).
4. Gautam Mathur; *Planning for Steady Growth*, Basil Blackwell, Oxford (1965).
5. B. Satyanarayan, *India's Trade with Asia and the Far East Countries*, BR Publishing Corporation, New Delhi (1986).
6. B. Satyanarayan, *A Comparative Study of Foreign Direct Investment in China and India*, (Edited) Himalaya Publishing House, Bombay (1996).
7. B. Satyanarayan, *Social Sciences and Planning for Sustainable Development*, (Edited) Himalaya Publishing House, Bombay (1997).
8. H. Myint, *The Economics of the Developing Countries*, (1965).
9. B. Satyanarayan, "An Analysis of Inter-State Disparities in India", *Economic Growth and Social Change*, New Delhi, March 1994.
10. H.B. Chenery, "Pattern of Industrial Growth", *American Economic Review*, Sept. 1960, (100).

7

Population Growth, Environmental Problems and Sustainable Development

> The central issue of our time may well turn out to be how the world addresses the problem of ever expanding human numbers.
>
> —*James Grant, Director General, UNICEF*

Projections made by the United Nations placed the World's population figure at more than 6.1 billion by the end of the twentieth century. More than 4/5ths of this population will be inhabiting in the developing world only. What will be the economic and social implications for the overall levels of living, national and personal esteem, freedom of choice if these projections are realised? Now the significant question is whether rapid population growth will become a serious problem only to the developing world or is it a manifestation of more fundamental problem of under-development and the unequal utilisation of global resources between the rich and poor nations. These and other questions lie at the core of the current world wide interest and debate about world population growth and human welfare. The main elements of the debate were clearly evident at the first world Population Conference held in Bucharest in August 1974.

Population Growth and the Quality of Life

Every year more than 80 million people are being added to a World population over 6 billion. More than 65 million of these additional people will be born each year in the Third World countries. The problem of population growth is not merely a problem of numbers. It is a problem of human welfare and of "development". If development entails the improvement in people's levels or. living—their incomes, health, education and general well-being, then the really important question about population growth is; How does the contemporary population situation in many Third World countries contribute to detract from their chances of realising the goals of development, not only for the current generation but also for future generations? Conversely, how does development affect population growth? In view of these questions, it becomes essential to frame the population issue not simply in terms of numbers or densities but more in terms of qualitative aspect of life. According to Bernard Berelson, Former President of the Population Council, "the qualities of human life: prosperity in place of poverty, education in place of ignorance, health in place of illness and death, environmental beauty in place of deterioration, full opportunities for the next generations of children in place of current limitations.... Population trends, if favourable, open man's options and enlarge his choices. Thus, population policy is not an end, but only a means —a means to the better life. That is what the concern about population is about, or ought to be".

At the beginning of the Christian era nearly 2000 years ago, world population had grown to nearly 250 million, less than half the population of India today. From AD 1 to the beginning of the industrial revolution around 1750 it increased two fold to 278 million people, less than the total number of those living in China today. During the next 200 years (1750-

1950), an additional 1.7 billion people were added to the earth's numbers. But in the last 40 years (1950-90) world population has more than doubled again, bringing the total figure as 5.4 billion. On this basis, the world's population is projected to almost 6.2 billion in the year of 2000. Some of these broad trends are shown in Table 1.

TABLE 1

Trends in World Population Growths

Year	*Estimated Population*	*Estimated annual increase in the intervening period*
1900	1,608,000,000	0.65 %
1950	2,486,000,000	0.91 %
1970	3,632,000,000	2.09 %
1980	4,390,000,000	1.7 %
1990 (mid-1992)	5,438,000,000	1.7 %
2000 (1992-2000)	6,113,000,000	1.5 %

Sources: Based on "United Nations Demographic Year book for 1971; Population Reference Bureau, 1979 and World Development Report, 1994.

In the twentieth century, conditions like famines, disease, malnutrition, plagues, wars etc., have been controlled. As a result, human mortality (the death rate) is lower than at any other point in human existence. It is this decline in mortality resulting from rapid technological advances in modern medicine and the spread of modern public measures throughout the world, particularly during the last 30-40 years, that has resulted in the unprecedented increases in world population growth especially in the third world countries. For example, death rates in Africa, Asia and Latin America have fallen by as much as 50% during the last 30-40 years, while birth rates have remained relatively high.

In short, population growth today is primarily the result

of a rapid transition from a long historical era characterised by high birth and death rates to one in which death rates have fallen sharply while birth rates, especially in developing countries, have not yet fallen much from their historic high levels.

It is also a fact that the world's population is very unevenly distributed by geographic regions, of the World's total population in 1990, more than two-thirds lived in developing countries, while less than one third in the economically developed nations.

There is a general argument primarily from the Third World countries, saying that:

(i) The problem is not population growth but some other issue;

(ii) Population growth is a false issue deliberately created by dominant rich - country agencies and institutions to keep LDCs in their under developed, dependent condition;

(iii) For many developing countries and regions, population growth is, in fact, desirable.

Many knowledgeable people from both rich and poor nations argue that the real problem is not population growth perse but one or all of the following issues.

(a) *Under-development:* People argue that underodevelopuent is the real problem, and development should be the only goal;

(b) *World Resource Depletion:* It is argued that an average North American or European consumer uses up, directly and indirectly, almost sixteen times as much of the world's food, energy, and material resources as his counterpart in Third World countries. The high fertility in LDCs is due to their low levels of live it is argued, which in turn are largely the result of the "over-consumption" of the world's Scarce resources by rich nations.

(c) *Population Distribution:* It is not the absolute numbers which is causing population problems but their distribution in space. What is needed is to reduce rural-urban migration and a proper spatial distribution of the population in terms of available land and other productive resources.

TABLE 2

Population of Various Regions in the World

Sl. No.	*Type of Region*	*Population (millions)*		*Per Capita GNP in dollars) (%)*	*Average Annual growth of population (%)*	
		Mid 1992	*2000*	*1992*	*1980-92*	*1992-2000*
1	2	3	4	5	6	7
1.	Low Income Economies	3191.3 (53.7%)	3654 (59.7%)	390	2.0%	1.7 %
2.	Middle Income Economies	1418.7 (26.1%)	1595 (26.1%)	2490	1.8%	1.5%
3.	High Income Economies	828.2 (15. 2%)	865 (14.2%)	22160	0.7%	0.5%
World		5438.2 (100 %)	6113 (100 %)	4280	1.7%	1.5 %

Source: World Development Report 1994, pp. 162 & 210.

Now, we shall have a look at the regional dispersal of population of the world; namely, Low Income, Middle Income & High Income Economies. These details along with their respective per capita incomes are shown in Table 2.

It may be noted that the Low Income Economies are having less $ 675 per capita income, while the per capita income of the Middle Income Economies are in the range of $ 676 to $ 8355. The High Income Economies have more than $ 8356 of per capita income per year. All these data pertain to the year 1992. All dollar figures are in current US dollars. Population numbers for mid-1992 are World Bank estimates.

It may be observed from table 2 that nearly 59% of the total world's population is living in Low Income Economies, which includes India and China, while 26% lives in the Middle Income Economies and only 15% lives in the High Income Economies. The rate of population during 1980-92 growth is 2% per annum in the Low Income Economies, while the growth rates are 1.7% and 0.7% in Middle and High Income Economies 'respectively. If we Compare the Average per capita GNP, its only a paltry sum of 390 US dollars in the Low Income Economies, while it is as high as 22,160 US dollars in the High Income Economies, which is nearly 57 times higher when compared to their underprivileged counterparts.

The population growth rates as projected by the World Bank during 1992-2000 are 1.7% for the Low Income Economies, while they are 1.5% for the Middle Income Economies and 0.5% for the High Income Economies. The overall trend shows that although the rate of growth of population is showing a declining tendency for all the three categories, the Low Income Economies should make all the efforts to bring it down to atleast 1.5% and ultimately to 1%. Only then, they will be able to improve their overall standards of living. Of course, along with this, they have to make efforts to raise their real national incomes.

Environment and Economic Growth

Conventional economic wisdom tends to focus on trade-offs as the basis for exploring the relationship between the environment and the economy. It suggests that environmental policy may conflict with cnconomic progress. Economic progress means both quantitative and qualitative progress in the context of clean and equitable improvements to socio-economic systems. Quantitative improvements enable us to meet the essential needs of the present generation without compromising the ability of future generations to meet their own needs. Qualitative improvements reflect our capacity to convert physical resource use into improved services for satisfying human wants.

The development and diffusion of environmentally sound technologies can change the way in which goods and services are produced and also generate benefits that can increase human welfare. The most promising areas for realising the gains of environmental technology today relate to energy use and the development of alternative fuels, to biotechnology and the development of agricultural practices that use fewer inputs and harmful pesticides, and to industrial production processes that reduce or present pollution.

Environment and Sustainable Development

The discipline of Economics thought that it had conquered the problem of unemployment in 1950's and 1960's, and turned its attention to the mysteries of economic growth, asking what would a long-term equilibrium look like and whether it would be stable or whether the economy would in the long-run be subjected to fluctuations and instability. In this whole exercise one fact was ignored. Some of the essential inputs were limited in supply. Ever increasing population and rising per capita income could not be accommodated with the earth s limited natural resources. Using a word that has become fashionable more recently, the question of the sustainability of the growth process was not properly addressed.

As people became richer, they found that the supply of produced goods such as cars and refrigerators was increasing compared to that of clean air or a quiet neighbourhood or open park land or unpolluted water. These environmental goods were becoming relatively scarce, but the demand for them was rising as real incomes rose. Since many of these goods could not naturally be increased in supply from the efforts of the private sector, there was a role for public sector.

The belief that environmental concerns were a rich country's preserve, and that tackling poverty was the paramount concern of developing countries remained the conventional wisdom for much of 1960s and 1970s. The change came about in the 1980s, when the key role of the natural resource base in the very process of development led some economists to emphasize the protection of environmental resources in the development plans of such counties and to seek the goal of sustainable development.

Debates about environmental regulation most often revolve around its economic consequences, particularly its effects on economic growth. Recently, this debate has become sharper. In addition to the "traditional" view that environmental regulation impedes economic growth (most often espoused by those in the business community) an opposing school of thought has developed. According to its proponents, not only can environmental regulation provide health and ecosystem protection, but it can stimulate the economy and enhance competitiveness at the same time.

The important points for sustaining healthy development of an economy are as follows:

(i) Although there is no ideal norm of industrialisation, the proper way is to take into account the impact of industries on environment;

(ii) The policy for environment should be set by proper discussion between the government and industrialists;

(iii) The people must be motivated to protect the environment;

(iv) Self-governance of local forests is a proper solution for protecting the environment;

(v) There should be some "greenmark" on environmental friendly products;

(vi) There should be high penalty for the country which produces more pollution. According to this, developed countries should pay to the developing countries, since they are producing more pollution. This point was raised in Rio at the Earth Summit, but USA has opposed it;

(vii) The population is the prime cause of environmental degradation. Because of this, the predominant lower castes including nomadic communities who directly depend upon natural resources are becoming more poorer;

(viii) Implementing land reforms and empowering rural and tribal communities to control and manage irrigation tanks, grazing land including forest areas alone will ensure the local communities the benefits available from these resources;

(ix) Natural resources are subjected to over-exploitation, congestion and degradation. Governmental intervention through fiscal instruments, revenue and expenditure is one of the solutions to arrest such resource use.

Finally, waste management is very necessary. It is better to try on reducing the waste itself. What is important is that environmental protection cannot be looked upon as an afterthought, it needs to be integrated into planning and costing of industries. Once this is accepted, the development is not only property sustained but the changes in economic policies need not also spell environmental disaster.

REFERENCES

1. Joseph J. Seneca *Environmental Economics,* Michael K. Tanssig Prentice Hall of India (1974).
2. D.W. Pearce, *Environmental Economics,* Longmans London, (1976).
3. Gregor, Howard F. *Environment and Economic Life.*
4. B.C. Tandon: *Environment and Entrepreneur* (1975).
5. K.D. Saxena, *Environmental). Planning, Policies and Programmes in India,* Shipra Publications, Delhi (1993).
6. Anil Markandeya (Edited) *Environmental Economics,* Julie Richardson Earthscan Publications Ltd, London (1992)
7. Malcom S. Adisheshiah (Ed), *Economics of Wasteland Development,* Lancer Press, New Delhi (1989).
8. A.K. Sen, *Poverty and Famines; An Essay on Entitlement and Deprivation,* Oxford, Clarendon Press (1981).
9. S. Chakravarty, *Development Planning; The Indian Experience,* Clarendon Press: Oxford (1987).
10. J.N. Bhagwati & P. Desai, *Indian Planning for Industrialisation,* Oxford UN: Press, London (1970).
11. Tarlok Singh, *Poverty and Social Change,* Orient Longmans, New Delhi (1969).
12. Gautam Mathur, "Economic Justice in a Free Society", Wiley Eastern Ltd., New Delhi (1994).
13. B. Satyanarayan (Edited) "A Comparative Study of Foreign Direct Investment in India and China: Problems and Prospects", Himayala Publishing House (1996).
14. B. Satyanarayan, (Edited) "Social Sciences and Planning For Sustainable Development", Himayala Publishing House, (1997)

8

New Economic Reforms and Role of Foreign Direct Investment in India

I

Growth with social justice has been the main goal of development strategy in India from the very beginning of planning. During the last four and half decades there has been impressive growth in the Indian economy but still more than 30% of the people live below the poverty level. The fact is that the absolute number of poor are still more than double when compared to what was at the time of Independence. The increasing population has neutralised the growth in the economy and the benefits of such development efforts have not percolated down to the rural areas. Moreover, the growth in the Indian economy has been relatively slow compared to many other developing countries. Sometimes, this state of affairs is attributed to both public sector failure or public intervention and market failure. Hence, the extent and quality of state intervention is a critical issue rather than the absence of or presence of government intervention in correcting market failure. The right choice for any country to develop on sustainable basis is to manage the resources more efficiently and to reduce dependency on outside finance for investment. But, it is always not possible especially when the internal economy is not strong enough to support accelerate growth.

Privatisation is often suggested as the alternative but has to kept in view that mere privatisation is not the panacea for overall development. Some sectors cannot be completely left to private sector despite fact that they are not doing well. The budget deficit keeps on increasing and also the inflation. This brought more improveshiment to poor people. It was also felt that due to many restrictions and rigidities industrial sector has not grown at desired rate. Hence, it became necessary to take some corrective measures to control the inflation, reduce the budget deficit and unproductive expenditure and liberalise the rules to create conducive atmosphere for overall development.

With this objective the new economic reforms were initiated in July 1991. Broadly, the New Economy Policy (NEP) has three main components of liberalisation, globalisation and privatisation, to create a more competitive environment in the domestic economy as a means to improving the productivity and efficiency of the economic systems. These policy changes relate to stabilisation policy and structural reforms. The stabilisation policies are intended to correct lapses in the short-run while the structural reform policies are intended to accelerate economic growth on sound footing. It is, therefore, necessary to supplement stabilisation policies by structural reform policies.

Since 1991, some policies such as: (1) Stabilisation policies to correct macro-economic balances; and (2) Structural reforms in the areas of industrial and trade policies have been initiated. The major objective of Stabilisation policies is to reduce the fiscal deficit. They included restraints on the growth of all expenditures, including social removal of discretionary controls, effective system of taxation, control of smuggling, and illegal dealings in foreign exchange, resource to IMF, free flow of foreign capital, devaluation of the rupee, changes in the EXIM Policy, raising issue prices of commodities, water and electricity rates are etc. The structural reforms were intended to transform the economy from agricultural to industrial economy from an inward-looking self-sufficient export-oriented economy, from a regulated to a deregulated economy and from a policy of nationalisation to that of privatisation. The package includes fiscal, exchange rate, trade and industrial sectors, the inflation rate is going is high and the prices of consumer goods, especially basic necessities, have increased considerably. However, there are divergent these new economic reforms, mainly on the rural poor.

The New Economic Policy is a set of policies and administrative procedures introduced in July 1991 to bring about changes in the economic direction of the country. It has two major components: Stabilisation and Structural reforms.

The stabilisation part has three components: (i) Management of Balance of payments; (ii) Controls of inflation; and (iii) Fiscal correction. Structural Reforms part has seven components: (i) Exchange Rate Adjustments; (ii) Liberalisation of imports; (iii) Rationalisation of Tariff Structure; (iv) Delicensing Restrictions; (v) Financial Sector Reforms; (vi) Disinvestment of Public Sector Shares; (vii) Foreign Direct Investment.

Though these policies and procedures have a macro-economic thrust, their impact on micro level economic activities cannot be ignored. From this point of view the New Economic Policy will have its repercussions on the entire gamut of economic development.

With this background, the present paper is devoted to discuss the problems and perspectives relating to only one sector, viz. The role of Foreign Direct Investment. Incidentally, this may also throw some light on the Human Face of

Development, in the sense as to how the resources which could have been invested in areas where FDI is allowed to flow in, could be diverted from being invested in areas which would help in raising the common man's standard of living. Now, we shall try to look at the details relating to FDI in Part II. It will give an idea as regards the total quantum, direction and the sources of FDI.

II

India's policy towards foreign investment, has generally been guided by the Industrial Policy Statements and the Five Year Plans. The basic approach to FDI was first laid down in the Industrial Policy Resolution of 1948. The thrust of the policy has been to welcome foreign investment on a selective basis while maintaining majority ownership and control in Indian hands.

Since 1970's, it was regulated through the Foreign Exchange Regulation Act (FERA) and the Monopolies and Restrictive Trade Practices (MRTP) Act. Although as a general practice the equity participation was limited to 40 per cent in priority areas, like export sector and the area of sophisticated technology, it was allowed upto 74 per cent. Since July 1991, as a part of the New Economic Policy the Government of India has embarked on a policy of attracting more and more foreign investment in the country to augment the resources availability in infrastructural and other critical areas of economy. A number of policy measures were taken to attract both direct and portfolio investment from foreign investor. The government liberalised its policy towards foreign investment to permit automatic approval for foreign investment upto 51 per cent equity in 34 industries. The Foreign Investment Promotion Board (FIB) was also set up to process applications in cases not covered by automatic approval. During 1992-93 additional measures were taken to encourage and the NRIs and Overseas Corporate Bodies (OCBs) were permitted to invest upto 100 per cent equity in high priority industries, export houses, hotels, hospitals, sick industries, hotels and tourism related industries. India signed Multilateral Investment Guarantee Agency Protocol for the protection of foreign investors on April 13, 1992. Provision of FERA have been liberalised since 9th January 1993 as a result of which companies with more than 40 per cent of equity will be treated at par with fully owned Indian companies. Among the new extension of rate of tax of 30 per cent in respect of short term capital gains to the foreign institutional investors (FIIs) and the permission given to foreign brokers to do business in India on behalf of FIIs.

TABLE 1

Foreign Direct Investment in India

(March 1980)

S. No		*Branches*	*FCRC*	*Total*	*Percent of Total*
1.	Plantation	10.0	38.5	38.5	4.1
2.	Mining	2.3	5.5	7.8	0.8
3.	Petroleum	10.5	26.3	36.8	3.9
4.	Manufacturing	21.9	789.7	811.6	87.0
5.	Service	15.7	22.8	38.5	4.1
	Total	60.4	872.8	933.2	100

Table 1 shows that foreign direct investment in India upto March 1980 was only of the amount of Rs. 933.2 crores out of which 87 per cent was invested in manufacturing. During 1988-90, total value of equity in foreign investment was of the order of Rs. 1270 crores. This shows that the inflow of FDI was not significant till the eighties.

The efforts at mobilising non-debt creating foreign capital inflows have now begun to yield results. In terms of approvals, equity investment proposals worth $3.6 billion (Rs. 11,000 crores) were cleared since July 1991 upto October 1993. About 80 per cent of these approvals are in the priority sectors such as power, fuel and oil refineries, metullurgical industries, transportation, industrial machinery and telecommunication.

The SEBI (Substantial Acquisition of Shares and Take-Overs) Regulations, 1995 were amended to permit the FIIs (Foreign Institutional Investors) to invest upto 10% in the equity of any Company, to invest in unlisted companies and to invest in debt securities without any requirement for investment in equity. The list of eligible FIIs was expanded to include endowment funds, University funds, foundations and charitable trusts/ societies with good track record. Table 2 records the Foreign Investment Flows into India.

TABLE 2

Net Investment by FIIs

S.No	*Period/Year*	*Amount (US $ Million)*
1.	1991-92	148.0
2.	1992-93	585.0
3.	1993-94	1634.1
4.	1994-95	1528.3
5.	1995-96	2035.6
6.	1996-97 (April-December)	2032.8

Source: "Economic Survey - 1996-97" GOI.

It may be observed that Foreign Investment has picked up from 1992-93 onwards. Although, it had a sudden jump to $ 1634.1 million in 1993-94, it has more or less stabilised during the subsequent years. Of course, it has again come down to $ 1528.3 million during 1994-95.

Country-wise break-up indicates that FDI approvals in respect of the USA, Switzerland, Japan, Germany, the U.K., the Netherlands, Australia, Malaysia, Singapore, Hong Kong, Sweden and Republic of Korea showed a quantum jump.

According to a survey, conducted recently by the Indian Council for Research on International Economic Relations, including 74 Indian firms having collaborations with US multinationals (mainly from manufacturing sector) the most important determinant for investment in India is found to be low wages. This is followed by a large size of domestic market and availability of cheap skilled labour. Local technology support and export to third country are also considered important factors.

Besides, the survey focusses that the US firms in India were reaping a profitability ratio of 16.4 per cent as against only 8 per cent in manufacturing sector abroad. The rate of return Indonesia was 13.04 per cent, Thailand 4.6 per cent and China 1.15 per cent. The highest rate of return in India was noticed in chemicals and non-electrical machinery.

In India, there is opposition to reform move towards globalisation and privatisation which is being considered a deviation from the long standing policy of self-reliance and quest for egalitarian society. Opening up the economy to MNCs and investments is being regarded as opening up the economy to foreign exploitation and giving away to the elite consumerism favouring the urbanite class ultimately creating dualism: the 'islands of development amidst the ocean of poverty'. According to a study, the rich-poor divide has widened up in India in the post-reform period.

The issues, which have come up with the liberalisation, move—encouraging FDI is as (1). From the fact that it is private, it will clash with the social goals in the country; (2). That it is large and oligopolistic and hence possesses market and bargaining power that may be used against the interest of the host country; (3). That it is foreign and may serve national interest of a foreign country; and (4). That it is western may transfer inappropriate know-how, technology, management practices or products designed with characteristics not needed in the LDCs.

The unforeseen vicissitudes in the move of history have placed before nations new options and new perceptions. The world is heading towards a 'new mix' of the systems in their fight against hunger and poverty. The iron curtains are being removed and windows opened up for fresh air of globalisation and interdependence. Be it Chinese, Indian, or Russian economies, the world has lived with plans and regimentation and there is a move towards reforms. Countries have shown signs of 'Plan weariness' and are opting for change. It is increasingly being realised that planned economies are incapable of bringing about necessary structural changes which could do away with the chronic slow growth path of the economies and hence are unable to deal with the problems of poverty and unemployment and underemployment. The Chinese success story in terms of 10 per cent GDP growth rate and India's breakthrough during the eighties, all have made a case for learning through mutual experience and globalisation; from 'inward-looking' policies to 'outward looking' policies. Here is no contradiction. The age-old infant baby, protect the child and free the adult'. Even historically we find that most successful outward-looking policies were preceded by a phase of inward-looking protection.

In India, we may suggest that the policy of globalisation may be accepted as a long-term goal but to caution against the immediate ill effects of globalisation, we have definite options before us. In other words, the strategy of development for our country should not be entirely market-oriented but it should not be essentially based on the philosophy of indicative planning (social sector planning) and we should gradually globalise the economy. Thus, before advocating for overall globalisation of the economy we should see that there is a mechanism which can easily transmit it the benefit of globalisation from one sector to another.

With respect to FDI we will have to ensure that the overseas investments are channelised to the areas which are most desirable and needed for pushing up the rate of growth and filling the gaps in the national economy and do not move to consumer sector catering for the needs of elite, and neo-rich giving rise to consumerism. Otherwise, it would become counterproductive in terms of social needs and requirements of welfare and injustices endemic with the capitalistic system. We will have to evolve reform with Indian characteristics like that of 'socialism with Chinese characteristics' in China.

REFERENCES

1. Sukhmoy Chakravarty, *Development Planning - The Indian Experience*, Oxford (1987).
2. The Economic Surveys: Govt. of India 1993-94,1994-95, and 1995-96.
3. *Reserve Bank of India Bulletin*, April 1995.
4. *Economic Times:* January 9, 11, 1995.
5. Jagadish Bhagwati, *India in Transition Freeing the Economy*, Clarendon: Oxford (1993).
6. C. Rangarajan: Maximising Foreign Investment in *Recent Development in India*, (1993).
7. CMIE, Bombay: *World Economy and India's Place in it*, Oct. 1984.
8. C.T. Kurien, *Global Capitalism and Indian Economy*, Orient Longman, New Delhi, (1994).
9. B. Satyanarayan (Edited), "A Comparative Study of Foreign Direct Investment in India and China: Problems and Perceptions, Himalaya Publishihg House, Bombay (1996).
10. B. Satyanarayan, (Edited), *Social Sciences & Planning for Sustainable Development*, Himalaya Publishihg House (1997).

9

Towards Regional Cooperation Among SAARC Countries

It is a fact that the rich nations are getting richer, while the poor nations are trying to stand on their own legs. The world as a whole has grown in constant dollars at 4.7 per cent a year on an average during the period from 1950 to 1990. The faster-growing group of countries are the middle income nations, including some of the less populous OPEC countries and also countries such as Argentina, Brazil, Egypt, Greece and South Korea. These countries have had about 5.8 per cent annual growth on an average. Next in the growth race were the centrally planned economies including China, Soviet Union and the East European nations, whose average annual growth rate was about 5.4 per cent. On the other hand, the poorest nations, such as Afghanistan, Bangladesh, Ethiopia, India, Indonesia, Pakistan, etc., had only 3.9 per cent as their annual growth rate, while it was hardly of the order of 1.5 per cent as far as growth of their per capita income is concerned. Thus, though the poorest nations are trying their level best to wriggle out of the rigmarole, their income gap with the rich nations is gradually widening.

One possible way to accelerate economic growth of the developing countries is through regional cooperation.

Enhancing intra-regional trade is an important instrument of this overall approach. The desirability and feasibility of South-South Cooperation is no longer a matter of conjecture. Countries of the South are not uniform of their level of development or resource endowment. The dynamic complementarities among the developing countries in resources skills, technologies and market opportunities have opened new vistas of opportunities among themselves. Well-conceived and properly implemented programmes in that direction would help countries of the South to reduce their dependence on the North as well as their vulnerability to external trends and pressures. South-South Cooperation has acquired definitive form and content during the past decade in the action programmes adopted at the successive NAM summits and by the group of 77 at the UN. The declaration and the programme of action on the New International Economic Order (NIEO) adopted by the UN in 1974, the UN Conference on Technical Cooperation in 1978, etc., are the stepping stones towards establishing a framework of economic cooperation among developing countries.

A good example of how the developing countries have learned to act together for mutual benefit is the establishment of Global System of Trade Preferences (GSTP) among themselves promoted by the group of 77 countries. This was in response to a crisis situation created by the fact that while the developed countries were dumping their manufactured goods in the markets of the developing countries, they were raising protectionist barriers against exports from the latter. The only way out of this crisis situation is to promote trade among the developing countries themselves. A major hurdle for South-South Cooperation seems to be the persisting information gap among developing countries of the potentials and possibilities of cooperation, the available skills, resources and needs in various sectors. This has quite often resulted in developing countries importing from developed countries when their needs could be met at much a less expense and more appropriately from among their own fraternity.

India has been particularly active in forging economic links with the developing countries. Its trade with other developing countries has expanded at a faster rate than with the developing countries. Between 1975-76 and 1983-84, India's exports and imports with developing countries grew at 14.3 per cent and 18.4 per cent annually, whereas the overall growth rates of exports and imports were 11.8 per cent and 14.7 per cent respectively. The South Asian Regional Cooperation covers important sectors of economic cooperation including agriculture, health, population, meteorology, postal services, rural development, scientific and technological cooperation, sports, arts and culture, telecommunications, transport, etc. The first summit held in Dhaka in December 1985 established an organisation known as the South Asian Association for Regional Cooperation (SAARC).

The South-South Cooperation, especially South Asian Regional Cooperation, is a new platform which has provided a new horizon for regional cooperation in South Asia. Such a forum, as is evident from the various deliberations of SAARC's meetings, has identified new areas of cooperation which will go a long way in strengthening the cooperation of these member nations.

The fundamental purpose of the organisation is to provide for active collaboration and mutual assistance among Bangladesh, Bhutan, India, Maldives, Nepal, Pakistan and Sri Lanka in the economic, social, cultural, technical and scientific fields. It is an arrangement to promote and strengthen individual and collective self-reliance in South Asia, to contribute to mutual trust, understanding and appreciation of one another's problems.

Let us now try to understand the broad characteristics of SAARC countries including the broad areas for economic cooperation.

It may be observed from the following Table 1 that except Pakistan, India and Sri Lanka, where the secondary sector's share is in the range of 20-25 per cent, all other countries of the SAARC region are hardly having their share of industry in the range of only 4-7 per cent. This shows that they are mostly dependent upon primary sector.

TABLE 1

Composition of GDP in SAARC Countries in 1984

(in percentage of total)

Country / Sector	*Agriculture*	*Manufacturing Mining and Electricity*	*Others*
1. Bangladesh	53.3	7.3	39.4
2. Bhutan	71.2	4.5	24.3
3. India	34.0	20.6	45.4
4. Maldives	29.3	6.7	64.0
5. Nepal	63.0	5.3	31.7
6. Pakistan	24.4	24.6	51.0
7. Sri Lanka	26.7	21.0	52.3

Source: World Development Report (1987) Washington.

The above mentioned study has on the basis of structural and sectoral growth perspectives, suggested the regional economic cooperation in the following areas:

(i) Agriculture is likely to be more beneficial to Bangladesh, India, Nepal, Pakistan and Bhutan,

(ii) Energy is likely to be more beneficial to India, Maldives and Nepal,

(iii) Manufacturing is likely to be more beneficial to Bhutan, Sri Lanka, Bangladesh, India and Nepal,

(iv) "Other" sectors are likely to be more beneficial to Bhutan, India, Nepal, Sri Lanka and Pakistan.

The trade flows among SAARC countries constitute a small fraction, which is of the order of 2-3 per cent of their overall trade. In the recent past, these flows have been fluctuating but showing a rising trend.

Areas of Cooperation

Thus on the major areas of cooperation which needs to be considered tinder the purview of SAARC as a priority area is the trade sector. Although there may seem competitiveness in the area of trade, there is scope for expansion of intra-regional trade in the SAARC region. More specifically, the trade in certain commodities which are being exported by some of these countries, can direct the region's efforts at collective self-reliance. For example, India's main items of

TABLE 2

Potential Areas of Sectoral Cooperation Among SAARC Countries

	Country	*Agriculture*	*Energy*	*Manufacturing*	*Others*
1.	Bangladesh	H	L	M	L
2.	Bhutan	M	L	M	H
3.	India	H	H	M	H
4.	Maldives	L	H	L	L
5.	Nepal	H	M	M	H
6.	Pakistan	H	L	L	M
7.	Sri Lanka	L	L	H	H

Note: H=High, M=Medium, L=Low.

Source: Identification of Sectors and Product Groups for Economic Cooperation in *South Asia* Report (Mimeo) by Arif A. Waqif, Administrative Staff College of India, Hyderabad (India).

exports of non-traditional items such as engineering goods and chemicals offer vast opportunity in the region.

It may be noted that nearly 50 per cent of the world's total export of tea was from India and Sri Lanka and in case of jute over 80 per cent share in world trade has been from Bangladesh.

There is thus no denying the fact that India can play an important role in the process of regional cooperation in this region. India is not only big in size and rich in resources but also has a strong industrial base. For example, India is the only exporter of engineering goods in the SAARC region. Similarly, the technology base of India is quite advanced in the region. Given the stage of economic cooperation among the member states, India can exchange its technology with the member countries thereby accelerating the process of economic development. This can take the form of readymade technology, technical consultancy and joint ventures in certain projects, such as fast growing construction activities in the region.

It is normally felt that economic cooperation in trade and industry is perceived as a sensitive area, primarily due to relative differences in the stages of industrialization, institutional and technological developments among the SAARC countries. It is also partly due to their existing international trade, investment and aid relations with advanced countries outside the region, while a country like Pakistan appears to be apprehensive of being dominated by a country like India.

The major items of exports and imports of the SAARC countries are as on the next page.

It may be observed that the export baskets of India and Pakistan are relatively more diversified and include non-primary product compared to Bangladesh, Nepal and Sri Lanka. On the other hand, the import baskets of Bangladesh, Sri Lanka and Nepal include mostly consumer goods, while in case of Pakistan and India imports comprise mainly of capital and intermediate goods.

As it is the intra-regional trade of the SAARC countries is on the lower side. But there is a scope for more regional cooperation given the diversified nature of the member countries. The table given below records the intra-regional exports of the SAARC countries.

TABLE 3

Intra-Regional Exports of SAARC Countries (1986)

	Country	*Exports (US $ million)*	*Percentage of total trade*
1.	Maldives	5.3	18.3
2.	Bhutan	n.a.	—
3.	Sri Lanka	58.4	5.0
4.	Nepal	56.2	38.7
5.	Bangladesh	53.9	6.1
6.	Pakistan	108.5	3.2
7.	India	224.0	2.2

Exports	*Imports*
1. Bangladesh	
Jute goods; Raw jute and mesta; Readymade garments; Frozen food items and leather.	Machinery and transport items; Wheat; Minerals; Fuels and lubricatns; Animal and vegetable oil and fats.
2. India	
Agriculture and allied products; Minerals, fuels and Lubricants; Textiles fabrics and manufactures; Gems and Jewellery; Machinery and transport equipment; and Non-iron manufactures.	Petroleum, oil and lubricants; Fertilizers and chemicals; Machinery and appliances; Non-metallic mineral; Manufacturers and Iron and Steel.

3. Nepal	
Readymade garments; Carpets; Pulses; Hides and skins; Raw jute and jute goods.	Petroleum products; Machinery and transport equipment; Textiles and yarn; Chemical and related products; and Iron and Steel.
4. Pakistan	
Cotton yarn; Raw cotton; Leather; Rice; Fish and fish preparations; and Cotton Cloth.	Machinery; Petroleum products and Chemicals; Transport equipment; and Iron and Steel and their manufactures.
5. Sri Lanka	
Tea; Clothing, and accessories; Mineral fuels; and Rubber.	Foods and drinks; Fertilizers; Petroleum; Machinery and equipment; and Textiles.

Source: RBI, *Report on Currency and Finance* (1985-86), Vol. 1.

It becomes clear from the foregoing table that the intra-regional export of Nepal in 1986 was as high as 39 per cent followed by Maldives whose export within the region was around 18 per cent. Both for Pakistan and India., this level was as low as 2.3 per cent. In future, there is a good scope for an expanding level of intra-regional trade which may pave the way for an overall regional cooperation.

REFERENCES

V.R. Panchamukhi, *et al.* (1987), *Savings, Investment and Trade in the Third World*, RIS for Non-Aligned and other Developing Countries.

World Development Report (1987), Washington.

Charan Wadhava, *et al.* (1987), *Regional Economic Cooperation in Asia, Bangladesh, India, Pakistan and Sri Lanka*, Allied Publishers.

George Rosen, (1985), *Western Economists and Eastern Societies*, Oxford University Press.

A.K. Singh (1973), *Impact of American Aid on Indian Economy*, Bombay, Vora and Company Publishers.

Arif A. Waqif (Ed.), (1987), *South Asian Cooperation in Industry, Energy and Technology*, Sage Publications.

Bela Balassa, (1961), *The Theory of Economic Integration*, Richard D. Irwin, Inc., Illinois.

———, (1964), *Trade Prospects for Developing Countries.*

Indian Institute of Foreign Trade, (1968), *Trading with the World: Country Profiles.* B. Satyanarayan, (1986), *India's Trade with Asia and the Far East Countries,* B.R. Publishing Corporation.

10

Trends in India's Exports: Problems and Prospects in the Context of Liberalisation*

The global scenario has changed dramatically in the 1990s. The collapse of the Soviet Union, the political developments in East Europe, the emergence of a single European political union, the formation of new regional trading blocs - like NAFTA (North American Free Trade Area) and APEC (Asia Pacific Economic Cooperation), and the emergence of a polycentric economic world have far-reaching implications for the world in general, and India in particular. Together with the global changes, India has embarked on a major reform of its economy with a complete overhaul of its industrial and trade policies, with a view to introduce greater transparency and liberalisation. This paper focuses on India's export performance in the sixth and seventh plans, in the context of the new economic policies, and the changed international environment.

Export Trends during 6th and 7th Five Year Plans

Export performance in terms of volume growth of less than 3% per annum during the Sixth Five Year Plan

* Also appeared in *Indian Panorama*, New Delhi, Jan-March 1998.

considerably fell short of the target annual growth of 9%. By contrast, volume growth in exports accelerated during the Seventh Plan and averaged 6.3% per annum as against the targetted annual growth of 7%. Although the share of exports in GDP has shown a rising trend since 1986-87, the performance for the Seventh Plan period as a whole has not been distinctly better during the Sixth Plan period from this perspective. The share of manufacture, which was around 53% in terms of value during the Sixth Plan period, rose to about 70% on an average during the Seventh Plan period. Table 1 shows the Export Performance during Sixth and Seventh Plans.

TABLE 1

Export Performance during Sixth and Seventh Plan

Item	*Sixth Plan (1980-85)*	*Seventh Plan (1985-90)*
(a) Exports as a per cent of GDP	4.9%	5.0%
(b) Value growth (per cent per annum)		
(i) In rupees	13.0%	19.8%
(ii) In dollars	4.5%	11.6%
(iii) In SDRs	10.0%	6.6%
(c) Volume growth (percent per annum)		
Target	9.0%	7.0%
Actuals	2.7%	6.3%
(d) Level of exports (annual average)		
In rupees crore	8,967	17,387
In dollars million	9,125	12,267
In SDRs million	8,251	9,821

Source: Foreign Trade Review, April-September 1991, p. 116.

We next come to the direction of India's foreign trade. The shape of the European Community and North America in our exports increased during the Seventh Plan period, while those of the OPEC and East European countries declined in comparison with the Sixth Plan period as a whole. Table 2 gives the direction of exports over three time periods -1970-71, 1980-81 and 1991-92 for the major categories of countries.

TABLE 2

Direction of Exports (Percentage Share)

Sl No.	*Region*	*1970-73*	*1980-81*	*1991-92*
1.	O E C D	50.1%	46.6%	57.9%
2.	O P E C	6.4%	11.1%	8.7%
3.	Eastern Europe	21.0%	22.1%	10.9%
4.	Developing countries	19.8%	19.2%	16.1%
5.	Others	2.6%	1.0%	6.3%

Source: The Economic Times, 9th September, 1993.

From the foregoing table, it is clear that the share of developing countries in India's export has changed marginally and come down from 19.8% in 1970-71 to 16.1% in 1991-92. The share of OECD (or developed countries) in India's total exports has been growing from 50.1% in 1970-71 to 57.9% in 1991-92, after dropping to 46.5% in 1980-81.

Our global trade pattern in the recent past is more or less in consonance with the political and economic developments world over. Exports to GCA (General Currency Areas) have increased. With the collapse of the Soviet Union and the growing turmoil in Eastern Europe, both our exports and imports have declined drastically with this region. As a result foreign trade in rupee terms has declined. One favourable aspect of this development is that we earn more hard currencies with higher exports.

EXIM Policy 1992-97

The current 5-year EXIM policy (1992-97) is a step in the

right direction. The policy is indeed transparent and easy to understand. Several complicated licensing procedures, quantitative restrictions and other regulatory and discretionary controls have been dispensed with to a great extent and freedom for the export and import with the exception of further pruned import and export negative lists has been ensured. The export-import procedures have been substantially simplified and streamlined with a view to ensuring free flow of exports and imports. The policy aims at globalising India's foreign trade with pronounced bias towards exports.

The EXIM policy not only provides full freedom for import of all types of capital goods, but also most of the critical inputs which go into production.

Thrust to Exports

The Government of India has identified 34 thrust areas to channelise exports in an optimal way. The exporting units from these areas such as marine product, horticulture, floriculture, jewellery, bicycles and granite are being provided infrastructural support and development assistance to capitalise upon existing strengths.

Development of supporting industry plays an important role in rendering the competitive edge to industries such as cotton textiles, food processing, leather and jewellery. Textile and fashion apparel have a strong export potential.

India also produces good quality cotton at competitive prices. The yarn spinning and fabric weaving industries segments are also well developed. With the strong base of cotton textiles, even synthetic textiles have better prospects of development.

Food processing also has high growth potential. Agriculture, horticulture, floriculture, and aquaculture enjoy inherent natural advantages. Grains, fruits, cutflowers, vegetables and marine products processing industry, has a very high chance of development. India can turn in to a major exporter of marine products, wheat, rice, coffee, rubber, tea, fruits, vegetables, mushrooms, tobacco, spices and cashew.

Poor infrastructure availability is the main constraints for Indian exports. Power is available at a very high cost and that too not adequately. Railways, ports, air, road, telecom and other facilities are of poor quality. Due to inefficiency in fund mobilisation, interest rates are very high in spite of high saving rates. Industries largely depending upon the same have a poor chance of competing in the global market. Hence, in spite of cheap labour and raw material cost, the metal and chemical industries may not find the going easy in the export market.

Exports in the Context of Liberalisation

In the context of the new economic policies, better technologies are needed to improve productivity, and make products cost-competitive. Domestic support prices for agricultural goods should be made more flexible, and aligned to international markets. Existing ceiling laws that don't allow large-scale plantation for exports should be amended suitably. Food processing technology also needs to be developed primarily in three areas—packaging, food preparation and extension of shelf life.

In computer software, thrust should be on offshore development and packaged products. This is one area where India can develop its competitive advantage, as it has a considerable pool of qualified professionals.

India should also strengthen her multilateral trade agreements. In a multilateral framework, it is easy to accommodate newcomers and new trading areas on the basis of competitive advantage.

Thus, keeping in mind the changed global scenario, as well as her new liberalisation policies, India needs fresh initiatives on the export front.

REFERENCES

1. Harry G., Johnson (Ed), *The Strategy for Rich and Poor Nations*, (1971).
2. Karl P. Sauraut, *The Group of 77*, (1981).
3. *World Development Report* - (1985).
4. B. Satyanarayan *India's Trade with Asia and the Far East*, B.R. Publishing Corporation, New Delhi.
5. Bimal Jalan, *Indian Economic Crisis: The Way Ahead*, (New Delhi), Oxford University Press (1991).
6. M. Wolf, *India's Exports*, Oxford University Press, New Delhi (1982).

11

Where Do We Go from Here?*

A developing country like ours is still faced with quite a large section of population, which is not only illiterate and below poverty line, but also either unemployed, under-empolyed or non-employed. The main focus of Indian Planning has been on growth and social justice. The mid-term appraisal of the Eighth Five Year Plan and the strategy adopted for the Ninth Five Year Plan, has raised the question of recasting development strategies in night earnest. The capital - centred and urban-oriented approach has not been able to make India either self-reliant or achieve removal of poverty or lessen unemployment and inequalities in the distribution of income to any significant measure all of which are the important objectives of Planning in India.

In India, given the population and its factor endowments apart from the existing manpower with all types of skills, the proper planning as regards public sector should have been only in the specified areas, such as Heavy-Investment Sectors including the scarce raw materials required for it, basic essential consumer goods and the equipment for producing them. There is no justification whatsoever to start public sector undertakings in any other non-priority sectors such as Luxury

* A Radio Talk by Prof. B. Satyanarayan, Hyderabad, 5th Sept. 1998.

consumption goods and equipment for producing them including the import-substituting industries in this field. If this type of perspective planning with relevant policy measures were to be adopted and followed, we would have been for better in having built up adequate quantities of heavy investment in the required proportions, thereby having truly attained the commanding heights including the defence. A glaring example of nonpriority area chosen for the public sector is that of Automobile industry; namely, Maruti-Udyog Ltd. Similarly, one could think of innumerable examples such as Five-Star Hotels, Refrigerators, Colour Televisions, VCRs, Deep-Freezes, Air-Conditioners, Pop-up toasters, Washing Machines etc. The investment in public sector undertakings catering most of these luxury goods and its equipment including the precious foreign exchange being spent on importing them, could have given us a very much stronger capital-base which in turn would have raised the minimum standard of living of the masses by providing employment opportunities to a much larger section of the population. On the other hand, the income and consumtion disparities seem to have become much more widened because of lack of proper perspective Planning.

Even after (50) years of Independence, there is no substantial improvement in the standard of living of the poorer and unorganised sections of population. In fact, it is estimated that even today nearly 30% of our population is living below the poverty line defined as a minimum physical subsistence. This only shows that the economic growth that had taken place in our country has not been sufficient enough to completely transform the economy into a developed state. The fruits of development have also not been distributed equitably among different sections of population. Only the well-off section of the society have been benefitted mostly by this development.

In spite of the establishment of production capacity and existence of growth potential in agricultural, industrial and other sectors, the economy is not growing, at a rapid rate. Price inflation is relatively higher than the economic growth rate. Income and consumption inequalities have increased.

Concentration of economic power in few hands has also increased during this period. The basic causes and gaps which have contributed to this state of affairs are the absence of proper institutional reforms in the economy and absence of proper strategy of development.

For example, in agricultural sector land reforms have not been properly implemented. Another gap in institutional reform is the absence of development of a labour organisation which will ensure that the direct benefits of investment expenditure in rural and agricultural sector reach the unemployed and underemployed labour to the fullest extent. At present, substantial part of the benefits of these investments are reaped by the contractors and middlemen and not the labour.

In the industrial sector although public sector has grown substantially and is supposed to occupy commanding heights of the economy, it has been only helping the private sector by providing Economic and social overheads to increase the generation of profits and surplus in that sector. This has resulted in increasing the concentration of economic power in few hands and in providing the luxury and semi-luxury consumption goods to the upper income groups in the urban and industrial sectors. The orientation of the public sector is not towards laying the foundations of future growth and use the existing potential exclusively for future growth but it is also acting as a partner with the private sector in frittering away the real scarce resources of heavy and basic industries like steel, machinery, coal, power and transport facilities in the production of goods which are consumed only by the rich 10-20% of the population. The production of goods which are required by the common people or poorer sections of population like sugar, coarse and medium varieties of cloth, low-cost housing, urban and rural transport facilities is not increasing at a substantial rate. This is because sufficient investments are not provided in spite of the increase in demand. Lack of demand is only due to the adoption of improper strategy of development in which the goods produced are either luxuries or or comforts for a small minority and the production techniques adopted are such that they result in employment to smaller number of people and in the generation of more profits and incomes to higher income groups. This process gets accentuated in the present context of liberalisation policy which we have adopted since 1991, unless we try to regulate it selectively by using proper monetary and fiscal policies.

We have been able to build up a diversified industrial and service structure. We have a large pool of skilled manpower and ample entrepreneurial capabilities. There is also a recognition that in many areas of activity, development can best be ensured by freeing them from unnecessary controls and regulations and withdrawing state intervention. At the same time, it is a fact that growth and development of the country cannot be left entirely to the market mechanism. Planning is necessary to overcome such limitations of the market mechanism. Planning is essential for macro-economic management, for taking care of the poor and the down-trodden, who are mostly outside the market system and have little asset endowment. The challenge is how best to effectively dovetail them together as complementary to each other. If this is not aimed at, democracy in this country may get endangered.

12

Trade Liberalisation among SAARC Countries: From SAPTA to SAFTA*

Political, strategic and economic trends in the later half of the twentieth century make regional and inter-regional cooperation among Third World countries as an essential input of their growth, development and security. There are obstacles to regional and inter-regional cooperation in the Third World. But, the hurdles have to be overcome so that forces of development and progress can be strengthened. Regional groupings promote liberalisation among the member countries and further the process of liberalisation towards the rest of the world. Hence, regional and inter-regional cooperation become policy imperatives for the Third World Countries.

The process of economic cooperation in the SAARC region has now taken firm roots. Even though, the pace of cooperation has been slow, nobody can deny the fact that the efforts for fostering cooperation are being consistently pursued. There is a growing conviction at various levels—political, intellectual, business community, and people at large that the benefits of cooperation are great as also the costs of non-cooperation. Further, some countries might be perceiving the benefits and costs much earlier than the others. The experience of the past

* Seminar Paper, 11-12 Dec. 1998.

decade of SAARC brings out that the right kind of perceptions in favour of increased cooperation in the region would emerge sooner or later.

Ever since the conduct of the comprehensive-study on Potentials of Cooperation in Trade, Manufactures and Services in the SAARC Region, a number of policy initiatives have been taken to foster economic cooperation in the region. A SAARC Fund for Regional Projects has been set up with a view to facilitating the conduct of feasibility studies for the regional projects, involving two or more countries. A SAARC Chamber of Commerce has been launched. The SAARC Preferential Trading Arrangements (SAPTA) is under active negotiation. SAARC cooperation in the field of audio-visual areas has been initiated. A consensus on the factors responsible for poverty and the measures required for poverty alleviation are being reached as a result of the report of the SAARC Commission on Poverty. Many propositions for cooperation in the field of science and technology are also emerging.

Trade Cooperation in SAARC

"Regional cooperation is a multifaceted process. The national perspective, the regional perspective and the international perspective signify its multiple facets. Success in regional cooperation is largely influenced by the nature of harmony that is inducted in these multiple facets. This harmony is fostered partly by conscious policy initiatives at the government level and partly by the removal of constraints that impede the process of cooperation" (V.R. Panchamukhi 1973).

One of the major areas of cooperation, on a priority basis, in the SAARC region is the trade sector. Myrdal (1968) pointed out that trade among the countries of South Asia provides a major potential path for marked expansion. Although there appears to be competitiveness in the area of trade, there is considerable scope for the expansion of intra-regional trade in the SAARC region, more specifically in certain commodities. Economic cooperation in trade and industry is perceived as a sensitive area, primarily due to relative difference in the stages of industrialisation, institutional and technological developments among the SAARC countries and partly due to the existing trade, investment and aid relations with countries outside the region (Satyanarayan B, 1993).

The value of exports of the SAARC region, increased from $ 14.36 billion in 1985 to $ 45.84 billion in 1995. Imports of the SAARC region, in terms of value increased from $ 22.18 billion to $ 49.30 billion, during this period. SAARC as a region, accounted for 0.91 percent of the total World exports and 0.97 per cent of the total World imports in the year 1995.

Three regions, namely, Europe, ESCAP and North and Central America together accounted for about 83 per cent of the total exports of the SAARC region, while two regions, namely; Europe and ESCAP together accounted for about 63 per cent of the total imports of the SAARC region, in 1992. Thus, most of SAARC's trade is with countries outside the SAARC region. Intra - SAARC exports accounted for 4.1 per cent of total SAARC exports while intra-SAARC imports accounted for 2.6 per cent of total SAARC imports in 1992. This indicates the limited role currently being played by the members of the SAARC region in their intra-trade relations. The Trade Intensity Index indicates that the low level of intra-regional trade in the SAARC region is due to inward - oriented import substitution policies and a high level of tariff and non-tariff barriers.

About 64 per cent of the intra - SAARC trade is accounted for by primary commodities (Arora 1997 and Aggarwal and Pandey 1992). India's imports of Live Animals for Food (SITC 001) are met entirely from the SAARC region. Similarly, more than half of the total exports of Eggs and Birds (SITC 001) of India are going to the SAARC countries. Sri Lanka is a major importer of Rice (SITC 042) from the other SAARC countries. India's exports of Fresh and simply preserved vegetables (SITC 054) to the SAARC region are quite significant. Pakistan and Sri Lanka are the major suppliers of fresh and dried fruits and nuts (SSITC, 057, 058) to the other SAARC Countries. Nepal, Pakistan and Sri Lanka are importing sugar and honey (SITC 061) from SAARC while India exports sugar and honey to SAARC region. The main coffee trade (SITC 071) in the SAARC region, is taking place between India and Bangladesh. The main exporters of Tea (SITC 074) in the SAARC region are Bangladesh, India and Sri Lanka while Pakistan and Nepal import tea from the SAARC region. Spices (SITC 075) are occupying an important place in intra-SAARC trade. Sri Lanka is the major importing country of spices in the SAARC region.

Feeding stuff for Animals (SITC 081) also emerged as an important item in the SAARC trade. The pattern of trade supports the hypothesis that there is a great scope for expanded South-South trade in agricultural commodities.

Trade Liberalisation Measures in the SAARC Region

SAARC member countries recognised that a preferential trading arrangement would be the first step towards higher levels of trade and economic cooperation in the region (SAARC). The Inter Governmental Group on Trade liberalisation formulated a draft Agreement to set up the SAARC Preferential Trading Arrangements (SAPTA) based on Sri Lankan proposal. The signing of the framework agreement on SAPTA at the Seventh SAARC summit at Dhaka in 1993 constitutes a landmark towards expanding trade among the member countries. SAPTA came into force in December 1995. It is aimed at giving a fillip to the intra-regional trade, which presently is very negligible.

In order to be successful, SAPTA must ensure that the tariff cuts as well as the reductions in non-tariff barriers go beyond those already exchanged under various other agreements such as the Bangkok Agreement, GATT protocol and GSTP. Further, SAPTA preferential rates need to be fixed as a certain percentage of MFN' (most favoured nation) rates so as to ensure the maintenance of regional preferences in the context of global trade liberalisation.

SAPTA makes provision for 'step-by-step' liberalisation of intra-regional trade. Under this agreement, trade barriers are to be dismantled gradually leading to the expansion of intra-regional trade. Tariff, para tariff and non-tariff concessions are to be negotiated product-by-product. The negotiations are to be conducted by an Inter-Governmental group. Concessions are on the basis of reciprocity and mutuality of the advantages. The level of development of the members, the pattern of external trade as well as the trade policies form the basis for the agreement.

The SAARC Preferential Trading Arrangements (SAPTA) is expected to play an important role in boosting intra-regional trade. According to the country perspective reports on SAPTA, this preferential arrangement would benefit SAARC countries due to the following reasons.

1. The countries can substantially reduce the transport and transit cost because of geographical contiguity among the members.
2. Capital goods produced within the region may be more compatible to the factor endowment of member states that those imported from developed countries.
3. The increasing competition among the member states would result in technical efficiency in existing industry

as marginal firms might be forced to reduce their cost.

4. As economic ties become stronger and countries become committed to common economic goals, political problems will gradually recede.
5. Regional cooperation may also pave the way for regional banks or corporations which might be influential in promoting regional investment in larger projects.

SAPTA is assuming great significance in the intra-regional trade enhancement in the SAARC region. India offered tariff concessions on 106 commodities, followed by 35 by Pakistan, 31 by Sri Lanka, 17 by Maldives, 14 by Nepal, 12 by Bangladesh and 11 by Bhutan. India offered tariff concessions ranging between 10 per cent to 100 per cent of the applied (MFN) tariff. The tariff concessions came into effect from 7 December 1995.

SAPTA is hailed as a timely step towards the liberalisation of intra-regional SAARC trade. However, there are some strategic difficulties in its practical implementation. Many of the commodities which occupy a prominent place in intra-SAARC trade have not been given tariff concessions while a number of commodities which are included in tariff concessions are in fact not traded. For example, India offered tariff concessions for 106 commodities but imported only 22 of these commodities. The product by product and step-by-step approach does not harmonise well with the across-the-board liberalisation strategy. Further, the trade regime of the SAARC member countries suffer from lack of transparency.

Trade liberalisation efforts regarding intra-regional trade promoted SAARC to undertake a step further towards the creation of a South Asian Free Trade Area (SAFTA). The committee on Economic Cooperation has been directed by the SAARC foreign ministers to set up an expert group to look into the action required to establish SAFTA. The decision regarding the establishment of SAFTA represents a 'historic' move of SAARC from 'preferential trade' to 'free trade'. SAFTA is to be created before 2005 A.D. preferably by the year 2000 A.D.

The Success of SAFTA Requires

(i) Tariff concessions and reduction of the average import tariff level;

(ii) Dismantling of various non-tariff barriers;

(iii) Relaxing the norms regarding the origin of products;

(iv) Expanding the trade in agricultural commodities;

(v) Extending MFN clause to all the member countries;

(vi) A common trade policy;

(vii) Mutual trust and reciprocity;

(viii) Greater understanding and friendly atmosphere in inter-country relations and above all;

(ix) The greatest non-economic factor viz., political will.

This task involves massive and committed work. Discussions initiated on some of these aspects, for instance, indicate that there are over 5,000 tariff lines in the international harmonised code of commodity classification. To reach the goal of SAFTA, SAARC countries would be required to add about 1250 products every year covering the next four years (Arora, 1997).

The list of tariff lines for concessions has to be expanded significantly. Harmonization of trade policies and procedures would facilitate trade liberalisation even further. This includes the visa regimes, import and export licensing procedures and customs duties. Free travel among the SAARC countries would go a long way in establishing people-to-people contact. Business and trade delegations would improve communication while conducting trade fairs on a regular basis would open the windows of product knowledge.

A detailed analysis of commodity-wise structure of production and exports would indicate the nature of complementarities that characterise the SAARC countries. Simultaneously, restrictive trade practices that impede the expansion of intra-regional trade would be removed. Institutional and credit facilities should be strengthened. An Asian Clearing Union would streamline the payments position among the SAARC countries. Countertrade practices, extension of aid and promotion of a healthy climate for joint ventures are also important economic measures for the success of SAFTA as part of the evolution of an Integrated Strategy for the promotion of intra-regional trade.

A South Asian News Agency should be established which would satisfy the long-pending need for exchange of objective information and dissemination of knowledge regarding the developments in the SAARC countries.

Regional cooperation in SAARC is poised to enter a dynamic phase through the launching of economic cooperation, particularly in the area of trade. However, intra-regional trade in the SAARC region is relatively very low compared to many other regional groupings of the World.

The Inter-Governmental Group on Trade Liberalisation formulated the framework for the setting up of the SAARC preferential Trading Arrangements (SAPTA), which came into force in December 1995. SAPTA aimed at boosting the intra-regional trade of the SAARC region by making provision for 'step-by-step' liberalisation of intra-regional trade.

The decision regarding the establishment of SAFTA represents a 'historic' move of the SAARC region from 'preferential trade' to 'free trade'. SAFTA is to be created preferably by the year 2000 A.D.

To reach the goal of SAFTA, the SAARC countries would be required to include about 1250 products every year into the list of tariff lines for concessions. It also requires the formulation of an agenda for trade expansion as well as the evolution of a Common Trade Policy, along with an Integrated Package of policy measures for accelerating and distributing the benefit of trade and growth among the member countries. Above all, it requires the greatest non-economic measures in the form of political will to streamline the linkages and maximise the gains from cooperation in the SAARC region.

REFERENCES

1. Aggarwal, M.R. (1979) *Regional Economic Cooperation in South Asia*, S. Chand & Co., New Delhi.
2. Gupta, Bhabani Sen (1986), *Regional Cooperation and Development in South Asia*, South Asian Publishers, New Delhi.
3. Gupta, Sisir (1964) *India And Regional Integration in Asia*, Asia Publishing House, Delhi.
4. Mukherji, I.N. (1990) *Trade Expansion in South Asia*, Macmillan India Ltd., New Delhi.
5. Muni, S.D. & Muni, Anuradha (1984) *Regional Cooperation in South Asia*, New Delhi.
6. Panchamukhi, V.R. (1993) "Regional Cooperation And Development" in D.K. Das (Ed) *SAARC-Regional Cooperation & Development*, Deep and beep Publications, New Delhi.
7. Satyanarayan, B. (1986) *India's Trade with Asia and the Far East Countries*, B.R. Publishing Corporation, New Delhi.
8. Satyanarayan, B. (1993) "Regional Cooperation Among SAARC Countries" in D.K. Das (Ed) *SAARC: Regional Cooperation And Development*, Deep & Deep Publications, New Delhi.

9. Wadhwa, Charan, D (1987) *Regional Economic Cooperation in Asia.*

10. Bhabani Sen Gupta (Ed) (1986) *Regional Cooperation & Development in South Asia*, Vols. I & II, South Asia Publishers, New Delhi.

13

Regional Cooperation in the Context of SAARC Countries

The term "regional economic cooperation" implies basically collaboration among a group of nations comprising the region on economic matters so that each member nation is able to derive greater benefits than what would be possible in the course of normal economic relationships without cooperation. Regional economic cooperation can take different forms. In a very narrow sense, the extent of cooperation among nations may be confined to specific or selected economic issues such as mutual trade agreements and preferential tariff. In a very broad sense, the scope of cooperation can cater to a wide range of economic issues like trade tariffs, technology, investment, joint ventures, fiscal and monetary policies. The benefits of economic cooperation are obviously greater when the level of cooperation is high so as to cover a large number of economic areas.

The impact of economic cooperation is also dependent on the nature of participation. At one level there can be cooperation among the governments of member countries on economic policy issues. At another level, there can be cooperation among the enterpreneurs and traders of member countries.

The terms 'economic cooperation' and 'economic integration' are sometimes synonymously used by analysts and policy makers. The concepts are distinctly different (Balassa, 1961). Regional economic cooperation is an evolutionary process consisting of several stages. Economic integration represents the most advanced or ultimate stage of economic cooperation. It is also some times pointed out that integral economic cooperation leads to increased economic integration and also growing interdependence. But these terms are loosely used in general discussions (Cooper 1980). As mentioned earlier, economic integration reflects a very matured stage of economic cooperation on the other hand, economic interdependence can arise based on the production and trade relationships established between countries and need not necessarily cover cooperation in other areas such as fiscal and monetary policies. In particular economic interdependence is sensitive to the economic developments within the concerned nations (Harris, 1991). In other words, economic integration usually leads to a high level of interdependence but increasing interdependence does not necessarily reflect economic integration.

The concept of economic cooperation is also some times interpreted in a narrow sense representing cooperation in trade in goods and services. The concept has however a very wide scope covering cooperation in the flow of factors of production like capital and labour as well as technology and information. If there are no restrictions on trade in goods and services, no constraints on the flow of capital, labour and technology and no impediments to the operation of competitive market forces, then exchange of goods, services, capital and technology among nations would take place in the course of normal business transactions between nations. The need for economic cooperation arises primarily because of the presence of restrictions on trade in goods and services and constraints on the capital and technology. The removal of this barrier is therefore the basic objective of regional economic cooperation. The gains from regional economic cooperation need not necessarily be confined to trade in goods and services alone. It can be extended to various other areas such as utilisation of natural resources like water, human resource development and protection of environment.

Regional economic cooperation is an evolutionary process encompassing several stages of harmonization of the economic policy framework of the participating countries although some view the different stages as various forms of economic cooperation (Hitiris 1991, p.1). Each stage reflects the extent of degree of cooperation lent by the member countries for the common benefit of the group as a whole.

Various stages of the evolutionary process can be described in terms of taxonomic classification as given in Table 1.

TABLE 1

Stages of Regional Economic Cooperation and Their Features

Stage	*Preferential Tariff Arrangements*	*Free Trade Among Members*	*Common External Tariff*	*Free Mobility of Factorsof Production*	*Harmonisation of Economic Policy*	*Unification of Economic Policy*
1. Trade Policy Coordination	X					
2. Free Trade Area (FTA)	X	X				
3. Customs Union (CU)	X	X	X			
4. Common Market (CM)	X	X	X	X		
5. Economic Union (EU)	X	X	X	X	X	
6. Complete Economic Integration (ed;	X	X	X	X	X	X

It could be noted from Table 1 that the evolutionary process of regional economic cooperation has an internal dynamic in the sense that the progress from one stage to the next higher stage is influenced by an increasing degree of economic openness resulting from increasing economic dependence among the participating countries. The main feature of different stages are described below.

Stages of Economic Cooperation

(i) Coordination of Trade Policies

The basic objective is to avoid discrimination in trade between the countries forming the group. This coordination usually takes the form of limited cooperation in terms of preferential tariff arrangements for selected commodities among the partner countries.

(ii) Free Trade Area

The number of commodities covered by preferential tariff arrangements is gradually expanded over a period of time and this process ultimately leads to the establishment of a Free Trade Area (FTA). The main feature of FTA is that tariff as well as quantitative restrictions of all kinds of commodity trade between participating countries are eliminated. This is in accordance with Havana Charter which defines as follows. "A free trade area shall be understood to mean a group of two or more customs territories in which the duties and other restrictive regulations of commerce are eliminated substantially all the trade between the constituent territories in products originating in such territories".

An important aspect of FTA is that all the member countries retain their own tariff against countries outside the group. In other words, there is no common external tariff since each country retains its own tariff against non-member (Balassa, 1961).

(iii) Customs Union

Customs Union is the next advanced stage of regional economic cooperation. The customs union is characterised by blocks of countries with free internal trade and with a common tariff for the outside world (Tinbergen, 1954). The Havana Charter defined this as follows:

> "A customs union shall be understood to mean the substitution of a single customs territory for two or more customs territories so that: (a) duties and other restrictive regulations of commerce are eliminated with respect to substantially all the trade between the constitutent territories of the Union; and (b) the same duties and other regulations of commerce are applied by each of the members of the Union to the trade of territories not included in the Union" (Article 44, Havana Charter).

Thus, besides the suppression of discrimination in the field of commodity movements within the union, the creation of a common tariff wall against non-member is the main feature of a Customs Union (Balassa, 1961). The Rome Treaty establishing the European Economic Community is based on the same concept of a Customs Union.

Jacob Viner extended the definition of Customs Union so as to include an explicit mechanism that would determine the allocation of customs revenue between the participating countries (Viner, 1950). This has been suggested to compensate the revenue loss of countries which might have had relatively high level of tariffs as compared to other countries in the Customs Union. There are advantages and disadvantages of FTA and Customs Union. The main limitation of FTA is that it provides the scope for some participating countries with low levels of tariffs against non-members to import goods from outside the region and reexport those goods to the other member countries which have relatively high levels of tariffs. This would cause a revenue loss to the latter countries. On the other hand, this problem does not arise in the case of

Customs Union since all the participating countries would have a common external tariff. The main limitation of a Customs Union is that it is likely to lead to a retaliation from other countries or other regional groups which might affect the exports of some member countries. It is also possible that, despite the adoption of a common external tariff, countries within a customs union may still impose certain non-tariff barriers that can affect the flow of intra-regional trade. Such non-tariff barriers can be eliminated to some extent when the participating countries progress further towards the establishment of a common market.

The Common Market represents a further advanced stage of regional economic cooperation. The mechanism of a Common Market eliminates all restrictions on factor movements apart from removal of all barriers in trade in goods and services among the member nation. A Common Market provides full scope for the operation of competitive market forces. Intra-regional trade within the Common Market would depend solely on comparative advantage in terms of cost of production based on especially natural resource endowments.

(iv) Regional Economic Union

Economic union reflects a minor stage of transition before a Common Market becomes a fully economically integrated community. In an economic union there is a greater degree of harmonisation of Economic policies in all areas, viz., agriculture, industry, transport, trade, commerce, fiscal and monetary areas. The progress towards complete economic integration depends on the willingness of national authorities of member countries to confer real powers on supranational authorities of the region.

(v) Regional Economic Integration

Regional Economic Integration represents the most

advanced and perhaps the ultimate stage of Economic Cooperation. At this stage, a regional authority is established which decides on all regional policy issues and also implements thorn. The member nations are represented in the regional authority and as such they become a party to the decisions of the regional authority. The decisions of the regional authority are binding on all the member nations and this abridges to some extent the sovereign authority of the national governments of the participating nations.

It is important to note that each higher stage of regional economic cooperation, which represents a higher level of economic openness and a higher degree of economic interdependence, increase the need for greater degree of 'harmonisation' of economic policies in order to achieve the common objectives of the member countries.

This process would, therefore, necessitate more intensive intervention in the domestic markets of all the participating countries. In other words, the success or failure of regional economic cooperation depends essentially on the economic policies. This implies that member countries have to subordinate their own national objectives to the common objectives of the group if there is a conflict between the two sets of objectives. This raises the crucial question about the objective of regional economic cooperation, i.e., why a group of countries are willing to sacrifice their national soverignity to some extent for the sake of economic cooperation among themselves. In general, the objective of regional economic cooperation among developed countries are different from those between developing countries. We confine our focus here to developing countries.

Rationale for Regional Economic Cooperation

Regional economic cooperation among developing countries is generally considered to make an essential contribution towards their economic development. The rationable for regional economic cooperation is based on a number of factors, including some which may not be considered as economic in nature. First, regional economic cooperation enables the participating countries to overcome the small size of their domestic markets which is particularly important for small economics that are faced with the problem of achieving 'threshold' levels in many economic and technological activities. Regional cooperation helps the member countries in achieving larger economies of scale in production and attain specialisation.

Second, regional economic cooperation enables the participating countries to make much fuller use of underutilised economic potential in terms of human, natural and technological resources. Regional cooperation provides the scope for the participating countries to expand existing industrial activities and also to start new ones. This helps in industrial diversification and in reducing economic dependence.

Third, regional economic cooperation enables the participating countries to exploit the potential of complementarities and also to establish strategic alliances between enterprises with a view to improve their competitiveness in global markets.

Fourthly, regional economic cooperation produces also spillover effects in other areas in terms of the increased levels of cooperation among service enterprises, academic and research institutions, professional technical experts and the common people. Thus, regional economic cooperation would provide the basic for wider cooperation in many other areas such as arts, culture, sports, education and other related fields all of which combined together would go to improve the quality of human life in the participating countries.

Globalisation and Regionalism

Most economists would agree that complete free trade in the world is the most desirable objective and that the present framework of global trading system is not necessarily the best. The basic concern today, however, is about the implications of regional blocks on global welfare. There are apprehensions that the formation of big regional economic groups such as the European Common Market and the North American Free Trade Area will till the balance away from multilateralism and lead to fragmentation of the world trading system (Bhagwati J., 1990, 1991, 1992). Some economists however, view regionalism as a means of achieving locally what seems impossible to attain globally (Dombusch. R, 1990, Krugman, P., 1992). Whether regionalism and multilateralism can coexist and whether regionalism can even advance the cause of multilateralism are issues that are still being debated.

There are, however, good reasons to believe the regional economic cooperation and integration especially among developing countries can greatly help in expanding world trade. Regional arrangements for trade and other types of economic cooperation can perform a functional role as complementary mechanism to the multilateral trading system. Thus, for example, the expansion of intra-regional trade along with the expansion of inter-regional investment of the East and South-east Asian countries was facilitated by meaningful economic cooperation between and among the Newly Industrialising Economies (NIEs) consisting of the Republic of Korea, Taiwan. Hongkong and Singapore as well as the countries belonging to the ASEAN comprising Brunei, Indonesia, Malaysia, Philippines and Thailand (Singapore is actually a member of ASEAN but is included in the NIEs for analytical reasons).

The establishment of new institutional arrangements or

strengthening the existing ones for regional economic cooperation among developing countries can also be viewed as their response to the increasing importance of the process of globalisation of the world economy a process that is characterised by features such as the technological paradigm the new sourcing practices of the global firms the crucial role of information flows facilitated by the rapid development in global communication networks global flows of private capital and the growing importance of trade in services.

The trend towards globalisation can also be explained in terms of both supply and demand factors. The supply side is driven by the rapid development and spread of technology related to production. The demand side is motivated by the fast change in consumer tastes in developing countries. Globalisation can therefore be viewed as a response to satisfy the needs of people who desire quality goods at cheaper prices.

The main motivation for the emergence for new regional trading blocs is the desire on the part of a group of countries to strengthen their national economies by relaxing different kinds of barriers to trade and other related areas. This is based on the perception that it is premature to envisage the removal of tradebarriers across all the countries or the introduction of free trade at the global level. On the other hand, the establishment of free trade or even that of preferential tariff arrangements among a group of countries can be expected to facilitate the process of industrialisation of the economies within the region. Such arrangements would ultimately lead to specialisation and regional economic integration based on utilising economies of scale for producing for the regional market as a whole.

There is also the apprehension that the formation of regional trading blocs, especially among industrialised nations, is likely to create unfavourable conditions for the expansion of trade-off countries outside such trading blocs. While regional trading blocs provide sustantial scope for expansion of intra-regional trade the strength of a region's growth dynamism depends very much also on the expansion and liberalisation of global trade. In other words, an open multilateral trading system has been and still remains, critical to rapid regional growth. Hence, regional economies would stand to gain if they reduce impediments to trade among themselves without discriminating against others outside the blocs and degenerating into stumbling blocs for the spread of multilateralism.

That the formation of regional economic groups does not contradict the principles underlying multilateralism is evident from the fact that the vary first United Nations Conference on Trade and Development (UNCTAD) held in the early 1960s envisaged the role of regional economic cooperation as a potential instrument for accelerating economic growth in the developing countries. The Final Act of the first UNCTAD Conference held in 1964 stated:

> "regional economic groupings integration or other forms of economic cooperation should be promoted among developing countries as a means of expanding intra-regional and extra-regional trade and encouraging their economic growth and their industrial and agricultural diversification with due regard to the special features of development of the various countries concerned as well as their economic and social systems" (UNCTAD, 1964).

It is also important to note here that Article 24 of the GATT Treaty has the provision that permits the establishment of trading blocs among countries which grant each other reciprocal trade preferences without remaining that they necessarily be extended to the rest of the countries. The implications of this provision is that the establishment of regional trading arrangements does not negate the spirit of multilateralism enunciated by the GATT Treaty.

In sum, multilateralism and regionalism are two processes that are not necessarily antithetical or antagonistic. Regionalism helps in stimulating the forces of competition within a region and the region's competitive edge in global markets. Regionalism can thus be a response to globalisation and at the same time stimulate the microeconomic forces that drive globalisation. Regionalism and globalisation can thus be and often are mutually reinforcing (Oman, 1994).

Approach to Regional Economic Cooperation Among SAARC Countries

There is considerable scope for enhancing the level of regional economic cooperation among SAARC countries which could prove mutually beneficial to all the member countries. The process of economic cooperation can help in accelerating the pace of industrialisation and economic growth in all the member countries without conflicting with their own national objectives and priorities. The externalities created by regional economic cooperation could more than offset some of the perceived disadvantages. The rationale for regional economic cooperation among SAARC countries is based on a number of important factors. These countries have been experiencing relatively low rates of economic growth as compared to other developing countries in East and Southeast Asia. But the people in the SAARC countries are having great expectation about improvement in their standards of living and welfare. Further delays in meeting the aspirations of the people can lead to socially disruptive situations which would affect both growth and welfare. Considering the constraints posed by the emerging tendencies in the world economy regional economic cooperation among SAARC countries provides a viable strategy for the collective economic development of the region.

The second, and perhaps more important factor is that there are small and relatively less developed countries such as Bangladesh, Bhutan, Nepal and Maldives in the SAARC group. These countries could not simply give up their socio-economic goals because of apparent economic unviability resulting from their small size of domestic markets. These countries are endowed with specific kinds of natural and human resources that could be efficiently utilised for the benefit of the entire region. However the efforts for forging closer economic cooperation in the SAARC region can succeed only by carefully examining and identifying the areas in which regional economic cooperation would prove most fruitful. This would help in developing a regional identity which is important for taking full advantage of the economics of geographical neighbourhood (Panchamukhi, 1994).

There are certain basic guiding principles which need to be followed for ensuring success in the efforts towards promotion of regional economic cooperation. These can be listed as followsi:

(i) Cooperation should be based on the principles of quality, equity and mutual benefit taking fully into account the economic and social disparities as well as the differences in the levels of development among the countries in the region,

(ii) Cooperation should involve a commitment towards the common goals on the part of all the participating countries with equal respect for each other.

(iii) Cooperation should be based on consultation, deliberations and consensus on all economic and other related issues.

(iv) Cooperation should complement and build upon existing bilateral and other kinds of arrangements among the member countries.

(v) Cooperation should be based on modalities of economic opennes and interdependence and should be consistent with the principles of multilateral trading system established by GATT.

In addition to the principles listed above there is also a clear need to identify the objectives of regional economic cooperation and formulate an appropriate policy strategy for achieving those objectives. The basic objective is to accelerate the process of economic growth in the SAARC region taking due care that this process helps in reducing intraregional disparities in the levels of income and standards of living among the member nations. Two aspects are considered important in this process. One is trade liberalisation and the other relates to industrial restructuring.

REFERENCES

1. Davinder Kumar Madan (1996) *Indo-Bangladesh Economic Relations and SAARC*, Deep & Deep Publications (New Delhi).
2. M.R. Aggarwal (1979), *Regional Economic Cooperation in South Asia*, S. Chand & Co., New Delhi.
3. A. Arif Waguif (Ed) (1987), *South Asian Cooperation in Industry, Energy and Technology*, Sagar Publications, New Delhi.
4. Jagdish Bhagwati (1969), *International Trade*, Penguin Books.
5. Bhabani Sen Gupta (1986), *Regional Cooperation and Development in South Asia*, South Asian Publishers, New Delhi.
6. Sisir Gupta (1964), *India and Regional Integration in Asia*, Asia Publishing House, New Delhi.
7. T.K. Jayaraman (1978), *Economic Cooperation in the Indian Sub-Continen*, Orient Longman, New Delhi.
8. I.N. Mukherjee (1990), *Trade Expansion in South Asia*, Macmillan India Ltd.. New Delhi.

9. S.D. Mini & Anuradha Mini (1984), *Regional Cooperation in South Asia*, New Delhi.
10. T.N. Devi (1994), *Socio- Economic Profile of SAARC Countries*, South Asian Publishers, New Delhi.
11. B. Satyanarayan (1986) *India's Trade with Asia and the Far East Countries*, B.R. Publishing Corporation, New Delhi.
12. B. Satyanarayan (1998), *Regional Cooperation Among SAARC Countries with Reference to Trade Prospects* (A Major Research Project Submitted to UGC, New Delhi).

14

SAARC Region and Its Pattern of Trade*

Introduction

The world's trends point overwhelmingly towards political independence and self rule on the one hand, and the formation of economic alliances on the other." Competition and cooperation have become the balancing acts in the global market place. Competition is a well-known fact, while the main thrust of cooperation, especially economic, is to carve out a piece of your world where you agree to cooperate with each other. Such cooperation not only harnesses and improves economic ties within the alliance but also gives better competitive capabilities in its dealings with the rest of the world. The transition towards this change is being driven by the economic forces of greater global interdependence on the one hand and the integration of regional markets on the other. The present phase of transition is characterized by some of the features mentioned below.

First, the globalization of production is based on increasing intra-industry trade and especially intra-firm trade among the Trans-National Corporations (TNC's). This is normally

---

* Also appeared in *Regional Cooperation in Indian Ocean*, ed. by PV Rao, 2001.

reflected in various forms of close trading connections, resulting from different types of commercial arrangements and distribution-cum-marketing mechanism. Globalization represents global competition leading to the emergence of global firms which consider the entire world as their market-place for taking decisions on aspects such as the origin of raw materials, splitting of production stages and processes of manufacturing as well as marketing and distribution of products.

The second feature is regarding the efforts made to expand world trade through a reformed multilateral trading system, which would replace the existing arrangements under GATT. The establishment of the World Trade Organization (WTO) is expected to introduce new multilateteral trading regime, the scope of which has been widened so as to encompass agriculture, textiles and clothing, intellectual property rights, services, foreign investment, etc. From the point of developing countries, the new system would provide greater opportunities and challenges for expanding the foreign trade. The third important feature is that economic cooperation is now dominating the agenda of almost all the countries, be they developed or developing. The industrialized countries are making serious efforts for evolving procedures for collective management of monetary policies and alignment of exchange rates, EU being the most recent example. The developing countries are also approaching for promoting regional interests by focussing attention on issues of trade, technology and investment.

The efforts to strengthen economic cooperation among the countries is reflected in the emergence of regionalism as a potential instrument for changing the pattern of world trade. Its importance is prominently seen in the formation of various kinds of regional trading arrangements such as the

European Union (EU), North American Free Trade Area (NAFTA), Asia Pacific Economic Cooperation (APEC), etc. The basic objective of such arrangements is to strengthen economic linkages based on closer economic cooperation so as to increase intra-regional trade and at the same time appropriate a large share in world trade.

The SAARC Region

A South Asia's regional economic organization, the South Asian Association of Regional Cooperation (SAARC) was established in December 1985 with seven member countries, namely Bangladesh, Bhutan, India, Maldives, Nepal, Pakistan and Sri Lanka. The fundamental purpose of the organization is to provide for active collaboration and mutual assistance among the nations to promote and strengthen individual and collective self-reliance in South Asia. These countries share a common colonial past and economic underdevelopment. Over one sixth of the world's population and about half of the world's poor live in this region. Economic development aimed at improving the welfare of the masses has been the major challenge facing these countries. In recent years there has been an increasing awareness that a coordinated strategy of development would facilitate the task of fully exploiting the potential of complementarities to mutual advantage.

All these SAARC countries have recently carried out major reforms in their economic policies with a view to meet new challenges emerging out of increasing globalization. These reforms, which are intended to enable the SAARC countries to integrate themselves with the global economy can also help them to achieve economic cooperation among themselves.

These reforms have provided a new set of opportunities, especially for the private sector in these countries for forging closer industrial and commercial relations. There is yet a vast scope for involving the business sector both public and private in joint undertakings in the region. There are well established private sector companies in some countries of the SAARC region possessing financial, technological and managerial capabilities.These are important assets that provide new avenues for joint production arrangements in many areas ranging from basic consumer goods to intermediate and capital goods. The cooperation should therefore serve to exploit the region's complementarity in natural resources, technology, finance, managerial talent and market and also encourage consultations among SAARC countries with a view to taking common positions in negotiations in international commodity markets and in dealings with countries that consume their products.

The SAARC covers important sectors of economic cooperation including agriculture, health, population, meteorology, postal services, rural development, scientific and technological cooperation, sports, arts and culture, telecommunications, transport, trade, etc. This paper analyses two main aspects of the trading pattern of SAARC countries. They are:

(i) Intra-regional trade among SAARC countries,

(ii) SAARC's trade with rest of the world.

(iii) SAARC's Trading Pattern.

One of the important characteristics of Asia is its rapid growth in international trade. During the period from 1980 to 1992, the average rates of growth of Asian merchandise exports and imports were 9.6% and 8.1% respectively, compared with the world average of 5.5% for both exports and imports. A quick look at the basic trade indicators of the SAARC region shows that the average annual growth of exports has increased from 6.5% in 1980-90 to 8.5% in 1990-95. Imports, on the other hand, also increased from 6.1% in

TABLE 1

South Asian Countries Trade Within SAARC and with World (US $ Million)

Sl. No.	*Country*		*Exports*					*Imports*				
			1990	*1991*	*1992*	*1993*	*1994*	*1990*	*1991*	*1992*	*1993*	*1994*
1.	Bangladesh	SAARC	60	80	45	55	60	257	255	382	480	628
		WORLD	1672	1687	2037	2277	2699	3656	3421	3731	4015	4900
			(3.6)	(4.7)	(2.2)	(2.4)	(2.2)	(7.0)	(7.5)	(10.2)	(11.95)	(12.8)
2.	India	SAARC	487	623	719	821	1002	97	95	194	99	130
		WORLD	17813	17872	18498	20258	24150	23990	19509	23227	21225	25529
			(2.7)	(3.5)	(3.9)	(4.1)	(4.1)	(0.4)	(0.5)	(0.8)	(0.4)	(0.5)
3.	Maldives	SAARC	7	10	10	11	12	18	23	27	30	39
		WORLD	52	54	40	35	48	138	162	191	193	222
			(13.5)	(18.5)	(25.0)	(31.4)	(25.0)	(13.0)	(14.2	(14.1)	(15.5)	(17.5)
4.	Nepal	SAARC	15	21	46	18	16	52	99	83	91	115
		WORLD	216	257	352	364	348	452	500	477	528	600
			(6.9)	(8.2)	(13.1)	(4.9)	(4.5)	(11.5)	(19.8)	(17.4)	(17.2)	(19.1)
5.	Pakistan	SAARC	122	125	241	127	147	89	88	98	121	126
		WORLD	5587	6494	7269	6701	7332	7383	8431	9375	9492	884
			(2.2)	(2.0)	(3.3)	(2.0)	(2.0)	(1.2)	(1.04)	(1.04)	(1.3	(1.4)

6.	Sri Lanka	SAARC	69	61	58	71	88	184	308	422	416	469
		WORLD	1895	1987	2488	2859	3322	2636	3061	3474	4005	5066
			(3.6)	(3.1)	(2.3)	(2.5)	(2.6)	(7.0)	(10.1)	(12.1)	(10.4)	(9.25)
	Total	SAARC	760	920	1119	1103	1325	697	868	1206	1237	1507
		WORLD	27235	28351	30684	32494	37909	38255	35084	40475	39458	45201
			(2.8%)	(3.3%)	(3.7%)	(3.4%)	(3.5%)	(91.8%)	(2.5%)	(3.0%)	(3.1%)	(3.3%)

Source: IMF, Direction of Trade Statistics Year Book, 1995.

Note: Figures in brackets represent the percentages share of SAARC countries exports and imports in its total world exports and imports.

1980-90 to 10% in 1990-95, thus showing the increasing export orientation of SAARC region as against the earlier inward looking strategy. Exports as a percentage share of imports has increased from 51.7% to 86.3% thereby reflecting the increasing ability to finance large volumes of imports and reduce adverse balance of trade. The average per capita exports have also risen from US$44 in 1983 to US$80 in 1993. The direction of exports of individual SAARC countries shows that except for Bhutan, industrialized countries are the major export markets, while for imports developing countries are the major source except for India and Pakistan which also depend on industrialized countries for imports.

If we observe the trends in exports and imports of the SAARC countries with themselves as well as with the world, we find that SAARC's exports and imports among themselves as a proportion of its exports and imports to the world as a whole has gradually risen from 2.8% in 1990 to 3.5% and from 1.8% in 1990 to 3.3% in 1994, respectively. This trend for all the countries may be observed from Table 1. Individually, the share of exports within the region to its total exports has increased for India; and Maldives, remained almost constant for Pakistan and declined for Bangladesh, Nepal and Sri Lanka. As for the imports, this share has increased for Bangladesh, Maldives, Nepal and Sri Lanka and remained almost the same for India and Pakistan.

Table 2 shows the top five export markets of SAARC countries. This throws light on the individual SAARC country's direction of exports. Likewise, Table 3 records the top five import markets of SAARC countries.

It may be observed that almost all the SAARC countries depend upon USA, UK, Germany and Japan to a very great extent for selling their exports. Other important countries are Italy, France and Hong Kong (H.K). Except for Nepal, where

India figures in the top five export markets, no other SAARC country is a major export market for the other SAARC countries.

TABLE 2

Top Five Export Markets of SAARC Countries in 1994

Sl. No.	*Country*	*Export markets*	*Total*
1.	Bangladesh	(1) U.S.A (34%) (2) U.K. (9%) (3) Germany (9%) (4) Italy (6%) (5) France (6%)	64%
2.	India	(1) USA (20%) (2) U.K (7%) (3) Germany (7%) (4) Japan (8%) (5) H.K. (6%)	48%
3.	Maldives	(1) U.S.A. (19%) (2) U.K. (23%) (3) Japan (8%) (4) S.L. (25%) (5) Thailand (8%)	81%
4.	Nepal	(1) U.S.A (34%) (2) U.K. (3%) (3) Germany (43%) (4) Switz (4%) (5) India (5%)	89%
5.	Pakistan	(1) USA (16%) (2) U.K (8%) (3) Germany (9%) (4) Japan (7%) (5) H.K. (8%)	46%
6.	Sri Lanka	(1) USA (32%) (2) U.K (8%) (3) Germany (8%) (4) Japan (5%) (5) Belgium (6%)	59%

Source: IMF, Direction of Trade Statistics Year Book - 1995.

Note: Figures in brackets show the percentage of exports to each country out of its total exports.

Let us now look at the top import markets in the SAARC region.

As far as imports arc concerned, we find a different picture. The important countries from which SAARC members are importing are Japan, Singapore, India and USA. Some of these countries are also importing from China and Malaysia.

A long term trend in intra-SAARC trade (export + import) shows that while trade growth within SAARC increased at a slow pace of 3.82% between 1980-90, it suddenly increased to 30% between 1991-95. SAARC's world trade experienced a growth rate of 7.32% between 1980-90, while its growth rate increased to nearly 13% between 1991-95. The share of intra-SAARC trade in its world trade actually fell from 3,2% in 1980 to 2.2% in 1990 and has increased to 4.3% in 1995.

TABLE 3

Top Five Markets of SAARC Countries in 1994

Sl. No.	*Country*	*Export markets*	*Total*
1.	Balgladesh	(1) Japan (8%) (2) H.K (10%) (3) India (10%) (4) S'pore (10%) (5) China (8%)	46%
2.	India	(1) USA (9%) (2) Japan (8%) (3) Germany (8%) (4) Belgium (6%) (5) U.K. (7%)	38%
3.	Maldives	(1) S'pore (47%) (2) Germany (2%) (3) India (11%) (4) Japan (12%) (5) China (7%)	69%
4.	Nepal	(1) India (17%) (2) S'pore(13%) (3) Thailand (13%) (4) Japan (12%)(5) China (7%)	66%
5.	Pakistan	(1) USA (10%) (2) Japan (9%) (3) Germany (8%) (4) Mal (7%) (5) Kuwait (6%)	40%
6.	Sri Lanka	(1) Japan (10%) (2) H.K (10%) (3) India(7%) (4) S'pore(7%) (5) France (6%)	37%

Source: IMF, Direction of Trade Statistics Year Book - 1995.

TABLE 4

Intra-SAARC Trade and Its Percentage Share in World Trade

Year	Intra-SAARC trade (exp+imp) (US$ mn.)	World trade of SAARC countries (exp+imp) (US S mn.)	Percentage of intra-SAARC trade in its world trade
1990	1457	65490	2.22
1991	1788	63435	2.82
1992	2325	71159	3.27
1993	2340	72969	3.27
1994	2832	83110	3.41
1995	4518	105178	4.3

Source: IMF, Direction of Trade Statistics Year Book, 1995.

The recent trends in exports and imports (1990-95) of SAARC region indicate that while intra-SAARC exports have increased by nearly 15%, SAARC total exports have increased by only 8%. As for imports, while intra-SAARC imports have had a growth of 23% total SAARC imports have increased by only 3.6%. This shows that SAARC trade within the region is growing at a much faster pace than its total trade with the world.

TABLE 5

Bilateral Trade (Export) Flow between South Asian Countries 1985-94

(US $ Million)

From/To	*Ban*	*Bhutan*	*India*	*Mal-dives*	*Nepal*	*Pakis-tan*	*Sri Lanka*	*World*
Bangaladesh								
1985	–	–	30	1	5	42	5	999
1990	–	–	22	–	7	23	8	1,672
1992	–	–	4	–	–	30	11	2,037
1993	–	–	13	–	7	26	9	2,277
1994	–	–	26	–	10	19	5	2,699
India								
1985	104	–	–	1	82	12	71	8,265
1990	297	–	–	5	40	43	102	17,813
1992	292	2	–	9	79	53	199	18,528
1993	392	5	–	7	79	56	299	19,964
1994	509	7	–	18	91	64 3	133	24,150
Maldives								
1985	–	–	–	0.04	–	–	5	23
1990	–	–	–	–	–	–	7	52
1992	–	–	–	–	–	–	10	40
1993	–	–	–	–	–	–	12	66
1994	–	–	–	–	–	–	12	48
Nepal								
1985	–	–	46	–	–	2	4	135

1990	1	–	14	–	–	3	-	216
1992	–	–	20	–	–	3	22	351
1993	–	–	17	–	–	1	25	389
1994	–	–	16	–	–	–	–	342
Pakistan								
1985	65	–	38	3	1	–	42	2,738
1990	103	–	49	1	1	–	69	5,587
1992	136	1	136	2	1	–	85	7,269
1993	105	1	53	1	–	–	57	6,701
1994	119	1	46	1	3	–	70	7,332
Sri Lanka								
1985	15	–	6	5	1	27	–	1,265
1990	10	–	20	7	–	32	–	1,895
1992	7	–	12	9	1	29	–	2,488
1993	7	–	13	10	1	37	–	2,846
1994	8	–	29	13	–	38	–	3,332

Source: IMF, Direction of Trade Statistics Year Book 1992 and 1995.

Table 4 records Intra-SAARC trade (exports and imports put together) from 1990 to 1995 and intra-SAARC trade as a percentage of its world market.

It can be seen from Table 4 that although Intra-SAARC trade as a percentage of its world trade is very low, still it is found to be increasing from 2.2% in 1990 to 4.3% in 1995. This shows that the SAARC's extra-regional trade has doubled in percentage terms in the first half of the nineties.

TABLE 6

Bilateral Trade (Import) Flow between South Asian Countries 1985-94

(US $ Million)

From/To	*Ban*	*Bhutan*	*India*	*Maldives*	*Nepal*	*Pakistan*	*Sri Lanka*	*World*
Bangaladesh								
1985	–	–	65	–	–	18	5	2,526

1990	–	–	7	170	–	2	70	8 3,656
1992	–	–	4	284	–	–	88	6 3,731
1993	–	–	3	480	–	–	90	7 4,015
1994	–	–	3	486	–	–	131	8 4,900
India								
1985	29	–	–	–	50	28	5	16,329
1990	15	–	–	2	15	45	22	23,900
1992	9	4	–	–	22	145	15	24,206
1993	13	3	–	–	19	46	17	22,493
1994	29	3	–	–	17	51	30	25,529
Maldives								
1985	–	–	0.08	–	–	0.4	6	70
1990	–	–	7	–	-	1	10	138
1992	–	–	14	–	-	1	12	191
1993	–	–	8	–	-	1	15	218
1994	–	–	24	–	-	1	14	222
Nepal								
1985	7	–	90	–	–	0.1	0.01	293
1990	8	–	43	–	–	1	–	452
1992	–	–	87	–	–	2	1	488
1993	8	–	67	–	–	–	1	545
1994	11	–	100	–	–	–	–	600
Pakistan								
1985	46	–	16	–	0.1	–	31	5,888
1990	38	–	46	–	1	–	37	7,300
1992	50	2	52	–	1	–	33	9,375
1993	38	2	67	–	1	–	41	9,492
1994	24	1	72	–	–	–	42	8,884
Sri Lanka								
1965	0.2	–	75	4	4	34	–	1,832
1990	9	–	118	6	–	51	–	2,636
1992	15	–	307	9	24	67	–	3,474
1993	9	–	252	11	28	63	–	4,311
1994	5	–	374	13	0.4	77	–	5,066

Source: IMF, Direction of Trade Statistics Year Book. 1992 and 1995.

Bilateral economic activity among the SAARC countries has not been very encouraging. Several factors not uncommon to the developing countries make the SAARC experience no exception to the pattern. India's economic preponderance, fear of Indian goods flooding the neighbouring markets, lack of compelmentarity, economic nationalism and political prejudices are some of the constraints on the growth of bilateral trade between one and another SAARC member. Tables 5 and 6 explain the pattern of bilateral export and import trade respectively among the individual SAARC countries for the period 1985-94.

An analysis of bilateral trade flows in the region shows that:

1. Bilateral trade flows among countries in the region are very small.
2. The chief exporter in the region is India. Its exports are mainly to Bangladesh and Sri Lanka followed by Nepal.
3. The major importers are Bangladesh and Sri Lanka followed by Nepal.

An important aspect of the economic structure of the SAARC countries is the relative importance of international trade for the individual economies and the structural changes in their trade. Export efforts, measured in per capita terms, are quite low in the SAARC regions as compared to the countries in the East and Southeast Asian regions. While the per capita exports among the ASEAN group ranged from $125 for Indonesia and Philippines to $450 for Thailand, the per capita exports among SAARC countries are quite low ranging from $20 for Nepal to $163 for Sri Lanka tod $173 for Maldives. Sri Lanka can, however, be considered as the most export-oriented economy in the SAARC region. A review of the export performance in the region reveals that almost all the countries have increased their share of exports in GDP during 1990s, compared to 1980s, showing the increasing importance of external trade. Further, the rise in exports has been much higher than the increase in imports with the result that the ratio of exports to imports has shown a perceptible improvement in most of the countries. The trend could be seen from Table 7

TABLE 7

Export Performance of SAARC Countries

S. No.	*Country*	*Period*	*Percapita exports (US$)*	*Rates (Percent)*		
				Exports to GDP	*Imports to to GJP*	*Exports Imports*
1	2	3	4	5	6	7
1	Bangladesh	1982-83	8	5.9	14.8	39.8
		1992-93	22	10.8	17.4	62.1
2	Bhutan	1985	50	11.5	34.9	32.9
		1993	100	26.6	38.9	68.4
3	India	1980-81	12	5.5	1o.3	53.4
		1993-94	25	9.1	9.6	94.8
4	Maldives	1983	79	NA	N.A	N.A
		1992	173	23.1	98.8	23.4
5	Nepal	1983-84	9	4.6	17.6	26.2
		1992-93	20	13.0	28.7	45.3
6	Pakistan	1980-81	33	10.5	19.3	54.4
		1993-94	54	13.2	16.6	79.5
7	Sri Lanka	1982	119	22.7	38.9	58.3
		1993	163	30.5	42.7	71.4

Source: S.N. Raghavan, *Regional Economic Cooperation among Countries*. RTS, New Delhi, 1995.

The improvement in the export performance in the SAARC countries could be explained by the change in the structure of exports. The share of primary commodity exports in total exports declined sharply in all the SAARC countries with a corresponding increase in the share of exports of manufactures. Except Bhutan and Maldives, the share of exports of manufactures is more that 70 percent in all the other SAARC countries. This is largely due to an increase in the exports of textiles, especially readymade garments in almost all the SAARC countries. It is interesting to note that even a small country like Maldives has ventured to export manufactures mainly through the exports of readymade garments. However, in the case of both India and Pakistan, the contribution of readymade garment exports to total exports of manufactures has been relatively small since both these economies have already more diversified structure of manufactured exports. Overall, although most of the SAARC countries have acquired greater export orientation during 1990s, they have mainly concentrated on exports of readymade garments, more or less replicating the strategy that has been followed by the East Asian Newly Industrialized Economies in the initial stages of their growth process. It may be difficult to ensure the continued success of this strategy in future due to the phased removal of the quota system for readymade garment exports over the next ten years when the existing Multi-Fibre Agreement System would be replaced by open competition.

A comparison of SAARC region's trade with world trade shows that overall share of South Asia in the world trade is negligible while there of SAARC's exports in the world exports has increased from 0.67% in 1980 to 0.91% in 1994, the share of SAARC's imports in total world imports has gone down from 1.25% to 1.04%. SAARC share in world Bade has thus remained constant at around 1%. The actual SAARC export and import figures and SAARC's exports and imports as a proportion of total world's exports and imports between 1980 and 1994 can be seen from Table 8.

TABLE 8

SAARC Trade as a Share of World Trade

(US $ Milion

	1980	*1985*	*1990*	*1991*	*1996-97*
1. SAARC Exports	12,959	15,375	27,235	38,269	—
2. SAARC Imports	25,051	28,384	38,255	44,316	—
3. World Exports	19,20,800	18,48,700	33,79,100	42,22,200	—
4. World Imports	19,99,100	19,35,200	34,66,200	42,78,200	—
(Percent)					
(a) SAARC exports as a proportion of world exports	0.67	0.83	0.81	0.91	—
(b) SAARC imports proportion of world imports	1.25	1.47	1.10	1.04	—
(c) SAARC share in world trade	0.97	1.15	0.95	0.97	3-4%

Source: IMF, Direction of Trade Statistics Year Book, and various years, Washington, D.C., IMF, Interna Financial Statistics Year Book, 1996, Washington, D.C. Note: SAARC countries excluding Bhutan.

Conclusions

From the above analysis we can draw certain conclusions:

1. In all SAARC countries, the ratio of exports to their GDP is rising. Except for India and Pakistan, the ratio of imports to GDP is also rising. This shows greater trade orientation in SAARC region.
2. As a result of exports rising faster than imports, the ratio of exports to imports in the SAARC region is rising (except for Pakistan), thereby gradually reducing the adverse balance of trade.
3. Intra-SAARC's exports and imports as a share of its total exports and imports are very small yet it has been gradually rising. As a corollary of this, intra-SAARC trade as a proportion of its world trade is rising. A point that deserves mention here is that though official statistics show low levels of intra-

SAARC trade, the unofficial trade between SAARC countries is nearly 4-5 times higher than the available official data.

4. SAARC exports and imports as a percentage of total world exports and imports are very small. While the former has slightly increased the latter has declined in the period between 1980 to 1994. SAARC trade as a percentage of world trade has remained more or less constant at 1% upto 1994, although recent data, i.e. 1996-97 show an increase by nearly 3-4%.

The measures suggested for expansion of intra-regional trade in the SAARC countries can be facilitated through - (1) supportive policies such as removal of trade restrictions, (2) widening the range of products covered by tariff/trade preferences, (3) provision of deeper reductions in tariff, (4) regional coordination of investments in selected fields and (5) identifying opportunities for efficient import substitution within the region.

Thus SAARC as a region can improve its trade with rest of the world by reducing competition amongst themselves and exploiting the benefits of complementarity, mainly through joint undertakings in the SAARC region both in public and private sector. Global firms would provide better competitive and marketing opportunities for South Asian goods.

With greater economic development in the South Asian region and wider scope for cooperation amongst countries through political and economic understanding, SAARC can become a major player not only in the Asian but also in the global economy.

REFERENCES

1. Aggarwal, M.R., *Regional Economic Cooperation in South Asia*, Chand & Co., New Delhi, 1979.

2. Gupta, Bhabani Sen (ed.), *Regional Cooperation and Development It South Asia,* South Asian Publishers, New Delhi, 1986.
3. Gupta, Sisir, *India and Regional Integration in Asia.* Asia Publishing House, New Delhi, 1964.
4. Mukherji, I.N., *Trade Expansion in South Asia,* Macmillan India Ltd, New Delhi, 1990.
5. Muni, S.D. and Muni, Anuradha *Regional Cooperation in South asia* New Delhi, 1984.
6. Panchamukhi, V.R., "Regional Cooperation and Development"- in D.K Das (ed.), *SAARC: Regional Cooperation and Development,* Deep and Deep Publications, New Delhi, 1993.
7. Satyanarayan, B., *India's Trade with Asia and the Far East Countries,* B.R. Publishing Corporation, New Delhi, 1986.
8. Satyanarayan, B., "Regional Cooperation among SAARC Countries" in D.K. Das (ed.), *SAARC: Regional Cooperation and Development,* Deep & Deep Publications, New Delhi, 1993.
9. Wadhva, Charan D., *Regional Economic Cooperation in Asia: Region Trading Blocs and Opportunities for India's Exports,* Centre for Policy Research, New Delhi, 1987.
10. Naisbitt, John, *Global Paradox,* First Avon Books, NY, 1995.
11. Satyanarayana, B., "*Trade Liberalization among* SAARC countries from SAPTA to SAFTA", paper presented at the national seminar's on "*Building Regional Cooperation - India's Role*", December 1998, under the auspices of ICSAC and India International Centre, New Delhi.

15

Financial Status of Andhra Pradesh*

Andhra Pradesh with a population of 6.65 crore as per 1991 Census, is the fifth most populous State in the country. More than 70% of the State's population lives in villages. The State's population for 1999 is projected at 7.51 crores.

As per the advance estimates for the year 1999-2000, the Gross State Domestic Product at constant (1993-94) prices is estimated at Rs. 79268 crores. Likewise per capita income at constant (1993-94) prices for the year 1999-2000 is estimated at Rs. 9424.

A Draft 'Vision 2020 Document' was released on 26th, January 1999. It is the desire of the Government to make Andhra Pradesh State the foremost State in the country in terms of growth, equity and quality of life. The basic thrust of the Vision Document is to make development totally sustainable. During the last four years, the State Government has launched several schemes. The Janmabhoomi programme embodies the principles of voluntarism, participation, transparency, accountability and promotes excellence in all walks of life. The quality and accessibility of primary education including the primary health care delivery systems have been

* Also appeared in *Fiscal Deficits of State in India*, edited by Janak Raj Gupta, 2001.

TABLE 1

Andhra Pradesh State's Gross Fixed Capital Formation for the Year 1991-92 to 1997-98

(Rs. in Lakhs)

Sr. No.	*Sector*	*1990-91*	*1991-92*	*1992-93*	*1993-94*	*1994-95*	*1995-96*	*1996-97*	*1997-98*
1.	Agriculture	66319	88894	93075	108232	116628	115671	119824	150267
2.	Forestry & Logging	2760	2690	3128	2287	2827	4683	7698	9890
3.	Fishing	3005	3503	4247	4749	3175	4979	7093	11004
4.	Mining & Quarrying	21950	19981	30815	28112	58295	28418	20243	21024
Primary Sector		94034	115068	131265	143380	180925	153751	154858	192185
5.	Manufacturing	173399	174317	215675	224824	401450	473687	591084	650151
6.	Construction	21711	42625	33298	26929	37735	36774	44729	88732
7.	Elect., Gas & Water Supply	58916	90269	64066	61375	115808	138162	131300	104325
Secondary Sector		254026	307211	313039	313128	554993	648623	767113	843208
8.	Transport, Storage & Communication	60178	43157	113366	131151	128281	144579	170799	194859
9.	Trade, Hotels & Restaurants	2489	2278	22166	22512	24307	35061	26605	13985
10.	Finance, Banking & Insurance	7700	14431	17500	21076	33422	54418	81045	120473
11.	Real Estate, Ownership of Dwellings and Business Services	110479	124651	143353	162438	175353	192904	202293	230688
12.	Public Administration	24616	31566	23985	35947	36480	37039	38124	47176
13.	Other Services	22802	21791	37429	52167	46263	46490	47142	47406
	Tertiary Sector	228264	237874	357799	425291	444106	510491	566008	654587
	Total	576324	660153	802103	881799	1180024	1312865	1487979	1689980

substantially improved. Self help groups in many sectors have been actively promoted and expanded. The developmental effort of the Government has a special bias in favour of women and disadvantaged groups.

Gross Fixed Capital Formation

Capital formation assumes importance in the context of policy making by the State and Central Governments. It acts as an indicator in the measurement of economic growth of State. It reveals the potentiality of the investments in the public as well as the private sectors and gives net addition of the assets created during the year. Table 1 records data pertaining to Gross Fixed Capital Formation (GFCF) of A.P. from 1991-92 to 1997-98. It may be noted that the GFCF in Andhra Pradesh has gone up from Rs. 5763.24 crores in 1990-91 to Rs. 16899.80 crores in 1997-98, thereby recording a compound annual growth rate of 17.24%.

TABLE 2

Percentage Change Over Previous Year in GFCF in A.P. and All India at Current Prices from 1990-91 to 1997-98

Sr. No.	*Year*	*A.P.GFGF (Rs. in Crores)*	*% change over previous year*	*All India GFCF (Rs. in Crores)*	*% change over previous year*
1.	1990-91	5763	30.34	124004	20.66
2.	1991-92	6602	14.55	136503	10.88
3.	1992-93	8021	21.50	158857	16.38
4.	1993-94	8812	9.86	183418*	9.97
5.	1994-95	11800	33.92	222459*	23.87
6.	1995-96	13129	11.26	290113*	25.50
7.	1996-97	14880	13.34	327090*	12.66
8.	1997-98	16900	13.58	357836*	9.40

Figures upto 1992-93 are based on series (base =1980-81) and figures from 1993-94 onwards are based on new series (base = 1993-94).

It is also a fact that GFCF of the A.P. State in 1996-97 was Rs. 14879.79 crores as against Rs. 327090 crores of All India GFCF. As per the provisional estimates the GFCF of A.P. State during 1997-98 stood at Rs. 16900 crores. The percentage change over previous year was 13.58.

The percentage change over previous year in GFCF in Andhra Pradesh and AH India at current prices from 1990-91 to 1997-98 is recorded in Table 2.

It may be observed that the year-wise change in GFCF for the State of A.P. is consistently higher when compared to All India during all the years under study except 1995-96.

State Government's Expenditure

The total expenditure figures of the State Government (both Revenue and Capital) are recorded in Table 3. It may be observed that the total State expenditure was hardly of the order of Rs. 117 crores in 1960-61, which was just 12% in the State Domestic Product. This has phenomenally increased to Rs. 23,764 crores in 1999-2000 which is nearly 30% of its State Domestic Product. The quinquennial figures are shown in Table 3.

The Government's overall expenditure has escalated to greater heights because it has undertaken a number of social and economic welfare schemes during the last 5-6 years. Some of the important schemes are shown below:

(i) State Population Policy Programme.

(ii) Chief Minister's Empowerment of Youth Programme (CMEY).

(iii) SC, SJ and OBC Welfare Schemes including Hostels.

(iv) A Comprehensive programme for Economic & Social Development of the Scheduled Caste Families (Mundadugu) schemes.

(v) Minorities Welfare Scheme.

(vi) Tribal Welfare Scheme; A Development Scheme for Tribal Families (Chaitanyam) Scheme.

(vii) Housing and Habitat Improvement Programme.

(viii) Poverty Alleviation Programmes.

(ix) Drought Prone Area Programme (DPAP), Watershed Area Programmes, Desert Development Programme (DDP), Integrated Wasteland Development Programes (IWDP).

TABLE 3

State Domestic Product and Total Expenditure of the Government of A.P. at Current Prices

(Rs. in Crores)

Year	*State Domestic Product of A.P.*	*Total Expenditure (Revenue + Capital) of A.P.*	*% of total expenditure to SDP*
1960-61	983	117	11.90
1965-66	1521	228	15.00
1970-71	2523	328	12.98
1975-76	4218	673	15.96
1980-81	7209	1409	19.54
1985-86	12879	3159	24.52
1993-94	58227	10541	18.10
1994-95	61491	12459	20.30
1995-96	64966	14301	22.00
1996-97	69188	16265	23.50
1997-98	68105 (P)	17745	26.10
1998-99	75530 (P)	21050	27.90
1999-2000	79268 (E)	23764	30.00

Source : *CMIE*, March 2000.

Note: (i) The figures from 1960-61 to 1985-86 denote Net State Domestic Product, while figures from 1993-94 to 1999-2000 stand for Gross Domestic Product. Hence, there will be some variation. But, this is unavoidable.

(ii) P stands for Provisional, while E stands for estimate.

Besides these, quite a number of other schemes have been started for the overall improvement of rural and urban areas. Hence the total expenditure is on the higher side.

State Government's Budget

Table 4 gives a total picture of A.P. Government's overall budgetary position. It shows both Revenue and Capital Accounts, thereby one can have an idea as to how the financial position is taking shape through time as far as A.P. is concerned.

The main components of current receipts are tax revenue, income from property households, grants and contributions. Total current receipts of the A.P. State Government has increased from Rs. 8250 crores in 1993-94 to Rs. 17,795 crore in 1999-2000 (Budget Estimates). Contrary to this, the receipts under capital account have shown a continuous declining trend from Rs. 21,656 crores in 1993-94 to Rs. 702 crores in 1999-2000, which is a serious matter to be reckoned with.

As far as State Expenditure is concerned, the main items under current account are: Salaries and Wages, Pensions and other Governmental Consumption including transfer payments to the rest of the economy. This has increased from Rs. 8018 crores in 1993-94 to Rs. 22,695 crores in 1999-2000, resulting in a deficit of Rs. 4900 crores during 1999-2000. As regards disbursements (expenditure) under Capital Account, it has risen from a low level of Rs. 2200 crores in 1993-94 to Rs. 7124 crores in 1999-2000. Capital transfers are the payments made to assist capital formation in other sectors of the economy such as Local Bodies, Corporations and Private Institutions.

The overall deficit (Current and Capital Accounts) put together has been continuously rising from a low level of Rs. 112 crores in 1993-94 to as high as Rs. 11322 crores in 1999-2000, except the year 1995-96, wherein there is a surplus of Rs. 63 crores.

TABLE 4

Budgetary Position of Andhra Pradesh

(Rs. in Crores)

S. No.	*Item*	*1993 -94*	*1994 -95*	*1995 -96*	*1997 -98*	*1998 -99*	*1999 2000*
1.	Revenue Account						
	(a) Revenue	8250	8583	10174	13200	15029	17795
	(b) Expenditure	8018	9322	10000	16177	19279	22695
	(c) Surplus (+) or Deficit (-)	232	-739	-714	-2977	-4250	-4900
II.	Capital Account						
(a)	Receipts	21656	5700	6551	549	502	702
(b)	Disbursements	22001	4965	5774	6106	6157	7124
(c)	Surplus (+) or Deficit (-)	-345	735	777	-5557	-5655	-6422
	Overall Surplus (+) or Deficit (-)	-113	-4	63	-8534	-9905	-11323

Source: Director of Economics & Statistics, Government of Andhra Pradesh, Hyderabad-4.

Most of the State Budgets would be always in the red unless they take hard decisions both in raising their revenues and also regulating their expenditure. Some suggestions are given below:

(i) Subsidy payments are either to be removed or atleast minimised, such as rice scheme being followed in A.P.

(ii) A sort of uniform tariff/pricing structure is to be followed or self-imposed in the areas of electricity, water, property tax, motor vehicle tax, etc.

REFERENCES

1. Gautam Mathur, "Basic Choices in Development," *Indian and Foreign Review*, 1 July, New Delhi, (1972).

2. Anil De, *Planned Industrialisation: An Approach to a Positive Strategy — Policy and Programme for India*, Hyderabad, (1968).
3. National Council of Applied Economic Research (NCAER), *Techno-Economic Survey of Andhra Pradesh*, New Delhi (1962).
4. Nadkarni, A.G., Development Potential of Andhra Pradesh, *Yojana*, May 17, (1970).
5. *Economic Surveys*, GO1, 1997-98 and 1998-99.
6. *Economic Surveys*, Government of Andhra Pradesh, 1997-98 and 1999-2000 (Finance and Planning), Planning Wing, Department.
7. *Economic Trends in Andhra Pradesh*, February 1989.
8. *Economic-cum-Educational Classification of the Budgetary Transactions*, Govt. of A.P., February 1999, Directorate of Economics and Statistics, Hyderabad-4.
9. B. Satyanarayan, *Development Potential of Andhra Pradesh, Yojana*, May 17, 1970.
10. ——, "Telangana Development: Problems and Possibilities;" *Indian Journal of Regional Science*, Vol. V, No. 2, 1973.
11. ——, (Co-Editor), *State Finances in India*, Delta Publishing House, Hyderabad (2000).

16

Scope for Intra-Regional Trade among SAARC Countries*

Today almost all the countries must accept the fact that they are part of the world economy. No country can escape is role in the system of independent trading nations. Is still a debatable point whether the degree of inter-dependence among nations is increasing or not. But it is fact that the world trade has grown exceptionally fast in the post-war years. On the whole, the forces working for economic interdependence among nations seem irresistible.

It is a fact that the rich nations are getting richer, while the poor nations are trying to stand up on their own legs. The world as a whole has grown in constant dollars at 4.7% a year on an average during the period from 1950 to 1980. The fastest-growing groups of countries are the middle-income nations, including some of the less populous OPEC countries and also countries such as Argentina, Brazil, Egypt, Greece and South Korea. These countries had about 5.8% annual growth on an average. Next in the growth race were the centrally planned economies including China, Soviet Union and the East European nations, whose average annual growth rate was about 5.4%. On the other hand, the poorest nations,

* Seminar Paper, New Delhi, Dec. 2000.

such as Afghanistan, Bangladesh, Ethiopia, India, Indonesia, Pakistan etc., had only 3.9% as their annual growth rate, while it was hardly of the order of 1.5% as far as growth of their per capita income is concerned. Thus, though the poorest nations are trying their level best to wriggle out of the rigmarole, their income gap with the rich nations is gradually widening.

One possible way to accelerate economic growth of the developing countries is through regional cooperation. Exchanging intra-regional trade is an important instrument of this overall approach. The desirability and feasibility of South-South Cooperation is no longer a matter of conjecture. Countries of the South are not uniform in their level of development or resource endowment. The dynamic complementarities among the developing or countries in resources, skills, technologies and market opportunities have opened new vistas of opportunities among themselves. Well-conceived and properly implemented programmes in that direction would help countries of the South to reduce their dependence on the North as well as their vulnerability to external trends and pressures. South-South cooperation has acquired definitive form and content during the past decade in the action programme adopted at the successive NAM summits and by the group of 77 at the UN. The declaration and the programme of action on the New International Economic Order (NIEO) adopted by the UN in 1974; the UN Conference on Technical Cooperation in 1978, etc. are stepping stones towards establishing a framework of economic cooperation among the developing countries.

A good example of how the developing countries have learned to act together for mutual benefit is the establishment of a Global System of Trade Preferences (GSTP) among developing countries promoted by the 77 countries. This was in response to a crisis situation created by the fact that while the developed countries were dumping their manufactured goods in the markets of the developing countries, they were raising protectionist barriers against exports from the latter. The only way out of the crisis is to promote trade among the developing countries themselves. A major hurdle of South-South Cooperation seems to be persisting information gap among developing countries of the potentials and possibilities of cooperation, the available skills, resources and needs in various sectors. This has quite often resulted in developing countries importing from the developed countries when their needs can be met at much less expense and more appropriately from among their own fraternity.

India has been particularly active in forging economic links with the developing countries. Its trade with other developing countries. Countries has expanded at faster rate than with the developed countries. Between 1975-76 and 1983-84, India's exports and imports with developing countries grew at 14.3% and 18.4% annually, whereas the overall growth rates of exports and imports were 11.8% and 14.7% respectively. The South Asian Regional Cooperation covers important sectors of economic cooperation including agriculture, health, population, meteorology, postal services, rural development, scientific and technological cooperation, sports, arts and culture, telecommunications, transport, trade etc. The first summit held in Dhaka in December 1985 established an organisation known as the South Asian Association for Regional Cooperation. (SAARC).

The South-South Cooperation, especially South Asian Regional Cooperation is a new platform, which has provided a new horizon for regional cooperation in South Asia. Such a forum as is evident from the various deliberations of SAARC's meetings, has identified new areas of cooperation which will go a long way in strengthening the cooperation of these member nations.

SAARC came into being at the first South Asian Summit held in Dhaka in December 1985. The fundamental purpose of the organisation is to provide for active collaboration and mutual assistance among Bangladesh, Bhutan, India, Maldives, Nepal, Pakistan and Sri Lanka in the economic, social, cultural, technical and scientific fields. It is an arrangement to promote and strengthen individual and collective self-reliance in South-Asia to contribute to mutual trust, understanding and appreciation of one another's problems.

Let Us now try to understand the broad characteristics of SAARC countries including the broad areas for economic cooperation.

TABLE 1

Composition of GDP in SAARC Countries in 1984 (in % of Total)

Sl. No.	*Country/ Sector*	*Agriculture*	*Manufacturing Mining & Electricity*	*Others*
1.	Bangladesh	53.3	7.3	39.4
2.	Bhutan	71.2	4.5	24.3
3.	India	34.0	20.6	45.4
3.	Maldives	29.3	6.7	64.0
4.	Nepal	63.0	5.3	31.7
5.	Pakistan	34.4	24.6	51.0
6.	Sri Lanka	26.7	21.0	52.3

Source: World Development Report (1987). Washington.

It may be observed from the foregoing table that except Pakistan, India and Sri Lanka, where the secondary sectors share is in the range of 20-25%, all other countries of the SAARC region are hardly having their share of industry in the range of only 4-7%. This shows that they are mostly dependent upon primary sector.

TABLE 2

Potetial Areas of Sectoral Cooperation among SAARC Countries

Sl.No.	*Country*	*Agriculture*	*Energy*	*Manufacturing*	*Others*
1.	Bangladesh	H	L	M	L
2.	Bhutan	M	L	M	H
3.	India	H	H	M	H
4.	Maldives	L	H	L	L
5.	Nepal	H	M	M	H
6.	Pakistan	H	L	L	M
7.	Sri Lanka	L	L	H	H

Source: World Development Report (1987). Washington.

Note: H=High, M=Medium, L=Low

Source: Identification of Sectors & Product Groups for Economic Cooperation in South Asia Report (Mimeo) by Ariff A.Waqif, Administrative Staff College of India, Hyderabad (India).

The above mentioned study on the basis of structural and sectoral growth perspectives, has suggested the regional economic cooperation in the following areas:

(i) Agriculture is likely to be more beneficial to Bangladesh, India, Nepal, Pakistan and Bhutan;

(ii) Energy is likely to be more beneficial to India, Maldives and Nepal;

(iii) Manufacturing is likely to be more beneficial to Bhutan, Sri Lanka, Bangladesh, and Pakistan,

(iv) "Others" sector is likely to be more beneficial to Bhutan, India, Nepal, Sri Lanka and Pakistan.

The trade flows among SAARC countries consume a small fraction, which is of the order of 2-3% of their overall trade. In the recent past, these flows have been fluctuating but showing a rising trend.

India's state trade organisations play a more significant role in her South Asian trade than in her trade with the rest of the world. However, they are involved more in exporting finished and semi-finished goods to the SAARC countries than in importing goods from them.

TABLE 3

Socio-Economic Indicators of SAARC Countries

Sl. No.	*Country*	*Population (Millions)*	*Per capita Income (US Dollars)*	*Adult Literacy*	*Life Expectancy at Birth (Years)*	*Infant Mortality*
1.	Bangladesh	101.5	135	26	46	136
2.	Bhutan	1.4	96	NA	44	150
3.	India	762.2	193	36	52	123
4.	Maldives	0-15	418	NA	NA	NA
5.	Nepal	17.0	145	19	44	150
6.	Pakistan	99.2	360	24	50	126
7.	Sri Lanka	16.4	340	85	66	44

It becomes clear that all the SAARC countries, irrespective of their size, population and industrial background, belong to the lowest strata of the developing countries of the world. The per capita annual income of Bhutan was as low as $ 96 while the highest per capita income of the region, $ 418, was enjoyed by the smallest country region, namely Maldives. India's per capita income was as low as $ 193, while Pakistan and Sri Lanka had about $ 350.

The present international economics situation characterised by stagnant economic growth, recessionary conditions and protectionist tendencies in the developed countries has seriously affected the growth prospects of the developing countries. The worsening terms of trade, acute balance of payments crisis and debt burden of the UDCs has further crippled the potential economic growth of these countries.

Under these circumstances the developing countries thought that it is better to unite themselves first and then negotiate with the developed world on equal footing.

Although South Asia as region is considered poor by way of conventional economic indicators, colonialism and imperialism of yester year explain at great length is present economic plight. While the population of the region is nearly 20% (about 900 millions) of the world population, its share in the world GNP is little less than 2%. As far as world trade is concerned, the share of South Asia in world exports was a mere 0.6% (about $ 12,000 million) in 1980, while its share in world imports was 1.2% (about $ 24,000 million).

Areas of Cooperation

One of the major areas of cooperation, which needs to be considered under the purview of SAARC as a priority, is the trade sector. Although there may seem competitiveness in the area of trade, there is scope for expansion of intra-regional trade in the SAARC region. More specifically, the trade in certain commodities, which are being exported by some of these countries, can direct the region's efforts at collective self-reliance. For example, India's main items of exports of non-traditional items such as engineering goods and chemicals offer vast opportunity in the region.

TABLE 4

Exports as % of Total World Exports of TEA

Sl.No.	*Country*	*1973*	*1979*	*1982*
1.	India	28.4	23.3	28.6
2.	Sri Lanka	29.9	25.2	21.0

It may be noted that nearly 50% of the world's total exports of tea was from India and Sri Lanka.

TABLE 5

Exports as % of Total World Exports of Jute

Sl.No.	*Country*	*1973*	*1979*	*1982*
1.	Bangladesh	—	70.3	81.4
2.	India	6.1	1.3	4.1

Source: UN Commodity Trade Statistics, (New York, UN 1971-84).

It was a fact that found around 86% of total jute exports was from these two countries.

There is no denying the fact that India can play an important role in the process of regional cooperation in this region. India is not only big in size and rich in resources but also has a strong industrial base. For example, India is the only exporter of engineering goods in the SAARC region. Similarly, the technology base of India is quite advanced in the region. Given the stage of economic cooperation among the member states, India can exchange its technology with the member countries thereby accelerating the process of economic development. This can take the form of readymade technology, technical consultancy and joint ventures on certain projects such as the construction activities in the region.

It is normally felt that economic cooperation in trade and industry is perceived as a sensitive area, primarily due to relative differences in the stages of indusrialisation, institutional and technological developments among the SAARC countries. It is also partly due to their existing international trade, investment and aid relations with advanced countries outside the region, which some small countries like Pakistan appear to be apprehensive about being crowded out by these Indian groups.

The major items of exports and imports of the SAARC countries are as follows. There is every possibility of exchanging each other's goods to their mutual advantage:

Sl.No.	Exports	Imports
1.	Bangladesh	Manufactures
	Jute goods;	Machinery and transport
	Raw jute and mesta	Wheat
	Readymade garments	Minerals, fuels and lubricants
	Frozen food items and leather	Animal and Vegetable oils and fats.
2.	India	
	Agricultural and allied products	Petroleum products
	Minerals, fuels and lubricants	Machinery and transport equipment
	Gems and jewelry	Textiles and yarn
	Machinery and transport	
	Equipment and non-iron manufactures	
3.	Nepal	Petroleum products
	Ready made garments	Machinery and transport equipment
	Carpets	Textiles and yarn
	Pulses	Chemicals and related products
	Hides and spins	Iron and steel
	Raw jute and jute goods	
4.	Pakistan	
	Cotton yarn	Machinery
	Raw cottons	Petroleum products and Chemicals
	Leather	Transport equipment
	Rice	Iron and steel and their manufactures
	Fish and fish preparations	
5.	Sri Lanka	
	Tea and mate	Foods and drinks
	Clothing and accessories	Fertilizers
	Crude fuels	Petroleum
	Mineral fuels	Machinery and equipment
	Crude rubber	Textiles

Source: RBI, "Report on Current and Finance", (1985-86), Vol. 1.

It may be observed that the export baskets of India and Pakistan are relatively more diversified and include more non-primary products when baskets of Bangladesh, Sri Lanka and Nepal include mostly consumer goods, while for Pakistan and India, the imports comprise of capital and intermediate goods.

As it is, the intra-regional trade of the SAARC countries is on the lower side. But there is a scope for more regional cooperation given the diversified nature of the member countries. The below given table records the intra-regional exports of the SAARC countries.

TABLE 6

Intra-Regional Exports of SAARC Countries (1986)

Sl.No.	*Country*	*Exports (US $ million)*	*Percentage of total trade*
1.	Maldives	5.3	18.3
2.	Bhutan	NA	—
3.	Sri Lanka	58.4	5.0
4.	Nepal	56.2	38.7
5.	Bangladesh	53.9	6.1
6.	Pakistan	108.5	3.2
7.	India	224.5	2.2

Source: World Development Report (1987). Washington.

It becomes clear from the foregoing table that the intra-regional exports of Nepal in 1986 was as high as 39%, followed by Maldives whose exports within the region was around 18%. Both for Pakistan and India, this level was as low as 2.3%. In future, there is a good scope for an expanding level of.intra-regional trade, which may pave the way for an overall regional cooperation.

Scope for Intra-SAARC Trade

Intra-regional trade among SAARC countries has been growing at around 27% per annum since 1991. It is now estimated to be more than $ billion a year. In the light of the operation of SAARC Preferential trading Arrangement

(SAPTA), the intra-regional trade by the turn of the century is expected to be anywhere around $ 10-12 billions. The trade turnover among the SAARC countries has gone up from $ 1820 million in 1991 to $ 2310 millions in 1992.

The Agreement on SAPTA aims at trade expansion among the members through exchanging concessions relating to tariffs, non-tariffs measures and direct trade measures. The SAPTA process has just begun with the member states exchanging their offer lists which has resulted in the first schedule of tariff concessions covering nearly 200 products. The agreement on SAPTA allows for various approaches to trade liberalisation such as product-by-product, across the board tariff reductions, sectoral approach and direct trade measures. So far, only the byproduct approach has made some progress. The modalities of SAPTA'S transition to South Asian Free Trade Association (SAFTA) are yet to be finalised. It is a fact that the intra-regional trade among SAARC countries still constitutes less than 3% of the region's global trade. While the global trade of all the South Asian countries has been rising, the share of intra-SAARC trade has not grown to the desired level. Of course, there is a good scope for an expanding level of intra-regional trade, which may pave the way for an overall regional cooperation.

REFERENCES

1. V.R. Panchamukhi et al, *Savings, Investment and Trade in the Third World*, New Delhi, RIS for Non-Aligned and other Developing Countries (1987).
2. *World Development Report* (1987), Washington.
3. Charan Wadhva et al., *Regional Economic Cooperation in Asia: Bangladesh, India, Pakistan and Sri Lanka*, Ahmedabad, Allied Publishers (1987).
4. George Rosen, *Western Economists and Eastern Societies*, Delhi Oxford University Press, 1985.

5. A.K. Singh, *Impact of American Aid on Indian Economy*, Bombay, Vora and Company Publishers (1973).
6. Ariff A. Waqif (Ed), *South Asian Cooperation in Industry, Energy and Technology*, Sage Publications, New Delhi (1987).
7. I.J. Ahluwalia, *Industrial Growth in Indian Stagnation*.
8. Bela Balassa, *The Theory of Economic Integration*, Richard D. Irwin, inc., Illinois (1961).
9. "__", *Trade Prospects for Developing Countries* (1964).
10. Indian Institute of Foreign Trade, *Trading with the World: Country Profiles*, New Delhi (1968).
11. Gautham Mathur, *Planning for Steady Growth*, Basil Black-well, Oxford (1965).
12. Raul Prebisch, *Towards a New Trade Policy for Development*, New York (1964).
13. Ignacy sachs, *Foreign trade and Economic Development of Underdeveloped Countries*, (1965).
14. Manmohan Singh, *India's Export Trends and the Prospects for Self-sustained Growth*, Calredon Press, Oxford (1964).
15. Paul Streeten, *Trade, Strategies for Development—Some Themes for Seventies*, Macmillan (1973).
16. B. Satyanarayan, *India's trade with Asia and the Far East Countries*, B.R. Publishing Corporation, New Delhi-52, (1986).
17. Debendra K.Das (Ed.) *SAARC Regional Cooperation and Development Perspectives, Problems and Policies*, Deep & Deep Publications, New Delhi (1992).
18. K.K. Bhargava etal., *South Asian Towards Dynamism and Cooperation*, ICRIER, New Delhi & Popular Parkasan Pvt. Ltd., Bombay-34 (1994).
19. B. Satyanarayan (Ed.) *A Comparative Study of Foreign Investment (FDI) in China and India - Problems and Perspectives*, Himalaya Publishing House, Bombay, (1966) pp. 254.

17

Economic Reforms and Human Resource Development*

I am pleased to get this opportunity of addressing this august body of academic-experts and policy makers assembled in this Seminar. The topic of the Seminar "Economic Reforms and Human Resource Development" is indeed very pertinent at this stage of country's development for intensive debate and discussions in the present times. I do not claim myself to be an expert in this field which has assumed very complex proportions in its scope and content in recent years. I am sure the specialized experts who have assembled here would discuss the various intricate issues that are of relevance to the conceptual and the policy dimensions of the topic. However, what I intend to do is only to cover a tip of the iceberg as a backdrop to the deliberations of the Seminar. I hope these would be found useful and stimulating for the subsequent discussions in the Seminar.

The concept of human development which was pioneered by the UNDP in 1990 attempts to go beyond per capita income in measuring the well-being of people. This it has done so by giving the health and educational status of the citizens of each country equal importance in the measure of well-being.

* Keynote Address Presented at Seminar in Hyderabad on 16 Sept. 2001.

According to the latest Human Development Report (2001), when it comes to progress in life expectancy, adult literacy, school enrollment and per capita GNP (the four indicators that constitute the Human Development Index). India's progress in 1990 has taken it to the category of countries with "medium human development". The bald truth is that both India and Pakistan come up poorly in whichever the component of HDI - Per capita Income, life expectancy or literacy.

According to 1996 Human Development Report of UNDP, during the years 1975-87, global gross national product grew by 40%, but this growth benefited a minority of countries. At the same time, the number of poor around the World increased by about 17%. As a matter of fact, the rich are getting more richer. Today, the assets of the world's 358 billionaires exceed the combined annual incomes of all the countries accounting for nearly half - 45%; of the World's people. One may wonder to note that the Industrial Countries (excluding East Europe and CIS) of the world are having an annual consumption of $ 16.5 billion (76%), while all the Developing countries of the world are able to enjoy an annual consumption of only $ 5.2 billion (24%) of the World. This disparity becomes more appalling when one looks at the items of annual expenditure which the World is indulging. The figures mentioned below are culled out from the Human Development Report of 1998: These are in terms of US dollars:

1.	Military Spending in the World	—	780 billions
2.	Narcotic drugs in the World	—	400 billions
3.	Alcoholic drinks in Europe	—	105 billions
4.	Cigarette Consumption in Europe	—	50 billions
5.	Business Entertainment in Japan	—	35 billions
6.	Pet Foods in Europe & USA	—	17 billions

7.	Perfumes in Europe & USA	—	12 billions
8.	Ice cream consumption in Europe	—	11 billions
9.	Cosmetics in USA	—	8 billions
10.	Basic Education for All	—	6 billions
11.	Water & Sanitation for all	—	9 billions
12.	Reproductive health for all women	—	12 billions
13.	Basic health & nutrition	—	13 billions.

This only shows the tilted balance which the present World is showing towards items of basic requirements like education, health, nutrition etc. If the expenditure on one item, viz., the military expenditure made by the countries of the World is diverted for some of the basic requirements the World would have been far better. Alas! The actual World Scenario is completely different. The picture becomes more glaring if we look at the below mentioned comparative Figures.

The Ratios of the richest to the poorest are :

(a)	Meat	—	11
(b)	Energy	—	17
(c)	Overall Consumption	—	16
(d)	Fish	—	7
(e)	Telephone lines	—	49
(f)	Paper	—	77
(g)	Cars	—	145:1

All these figures show that divergence between the Developed and Developing Countries is gradually increasing year after year. The disparities are so enormous. One could as well observe these differences region-wise at the global level for various economic indicators.

The table given below records some important items.

TABLE 1

Per Capita/Availability in 1995

Sl. No.	*Region*	*Calories per capi tal per day*	*Tele-phones per 1000 people*	*Petrol Kg. Per capita*	*Cars (1993) per 1000 people*	*Total Energy Kg of Oil equivalent per capita (1994)*
1	2	3	4	5	6	7
1	Sub-Saharan Africa	2237	12	27	11	458
2	Arab States	2903	49	113	42	1215
3	South Asia	2385	16	10	5	360
4	East Asia	2717	49	29	6	794
5.	SE Asia &. Pacific	2533	29	39	18	619
6	L. America & Caribbean	2781	86	152	61	1144
7	All Developing Countries	2572	39	43	16	670
8	Industrial Countries	3157	414	500	405	4568

Source: "Human Development Report", (1998).

It may be observed from Table 1 that the Developing Countries on the whole are having only 39 Telephones (on an average) per 1000 people, while the Developed World is having 414 per 1000 people. Likewise, we can compare other important amenities like per capita petrol consumption, cars and energy used etc.

I don't like to prolong the discussion at this rate endlessly; I shall try to throw light only on one item, which is so important to the humanity as a whole, viz., health. Health expenditure of any Country is a fair indicator of the well-being of its people. A wide divergence is discernible between nations in the matter of health expenditure. While the high income group spent more than $ 2500 per capita on health or ten percent of its GDP during 1990-97, the low income countries hardly spent $ 15 per capita (4.5% of GDP), just above the estimated $ 12 a year needed to secure the minimum preventive and essential clinical services. For example, the US spent an average $ 4000 per capita during 1990-97.

18

Economic Reforms and Their Impact on the Indian Economy*

In the context of the constitutional imperative of ensuring economic eouality under a democratic set up, the basic focus of Indian Planning has been on growth and social justice. The mid-term appraisal of the IXth Five Year Plan and the need to explore proper economic strategies for the ensuing Xth Plan with the objectives of abolishing poverty and achieving full employment, has raised the question of recasting development strategies in right earnest. The experiences of Indian planning dispel the hypothesis of growth process promoting employment.

A developing country like ours is still faced with a large section of population, which is not only illiterate and below poverty line, but also either underemployed or non-employed. The capital-centred, urban-oriented and non-selective hi-tech approach has not been able to make India either self-reliant or active for removal of poverty or lessen unemployment and inequalities in the distribution of income to any significant measure, all of which are important objectives of Indian Planning. The move towards liberalised economic policies in India in the recent past arising out of the logic of competition

* Keynote Address, National Seminar, Anantapur, 27 March 2002.

has led, given the pattern of income distribution in the context of mixed economy, to profit-seeking investment in consumer's durables and luxury consumables demanded by the upper and middle income groups. It has also resulted in import of repetive technology and increasing debt-trip.

Development Planning in India

In India, given the population and its factor endowments apart from the existing manpower with all types of skills, the proper planning as regards public sector should have been only in the specified areas, such as Heavy Investment Sectors including the scarce raw materials required for it, basic essential consumer goods and the equipment for producing them. There is no justification whatsoever to start public sector undertakings in any other non-priority sectors such as Luxury consumption goods and equipment for producing them including the import-substituting industries in this field. If this type of perspective planning with relevent policy measures were to be adopted and followed, we would have been far better in having built up adequate quantities of heavy investment in the required proportions, thereby having truly attained the commanding heights including the defence. A glaring example of non-priority area chosen for the public sector is that of Automobile industry; namely; Maruti-Udyog Ltd. Similarly, one could think of innumerable examples such as Five-star Hotels, Refrigerators, Colour Televisions, VCRs, Deep-Freezers, Air-Conditioners, Bop-up toasters. Washing Machines etc. The Investment in Public Sector Undertakings catering most of these luxury goods and its equipment including the precious foreign exchange being spent on importing them, could have given us a very much stronger capital -base which in turn would have raised the minimum standard of living of the masses by providing employment opportunities to a much larger section of the population. On the other hand, the income and consumption disparities seen to have become much more widened because of lack of proper perspective planning.

In spite of the establishment of production capacity and existence of growth potential in agricultural, industrial and other sectors, the economy is not growing at a rapid rate. Income and consumption inequalities have increased.

Concentration of economic power in few hands has also increased during this period. The basic causes and gaps which have contributed to this state of affairs are the absence of proper institutional reforms in the economy and absence of proper strategy of development.

For example, in agricultural sector land reforms have not been properly implemented. Another gap in institutional reforms is the absence of development of a labour organisation which will ensure that the direct benefit of investment expenditure in rural and agricultural sector each the unemployed and underemployed labour to the fullest extent. At present, substantial part of the benefits of these investments are reaped by the contractors and middlemen and not the labour.

In the industrial sector although public sector has grown substantially and is supposed to occupy commanding heights of the economy, it has been only helping the private sector by providing economic and social overheads to increase the generation of profits and surplus in that sector. This has resulted in increasing the concentration of economic power in few hands and in providing the luxury and self-luxury consumption goods to the upper income groups in the urban and Industrial sectors. The orientation of the public sector is not towards laying the foundations of future growth and use the existing potential exclusively for future growth but it is also acting as a partner with the private sector in frittering away the real scarce resources of heavy and basic industries like steel, machinery, coal, power and transport facilities in the production of goods which are consumed only by the rich 20—25% of the population. The production of goods which are required by the common people or poorer sections of population like sugar, coarse and medium varieties of cloth, low-cost housing, urban and rural transport facilities is not increasing at a substantial rate. This is because sufficient investments are not provided in spite of the increase in demand. Lack of demand is only due to the adoption of improper strategy of development in which the goods produced are either luxuries or comforts for a small minority and the production techniques adopted are such that they result in employment to smaller number of people and in the generation of more profits and incomes to higher income groups. This process gets accentuated in the present context of liberalisation policy which we have adopted since 1991, unless we try to regulate it selectively by using proper monetary and fiscal policies.

We have been able to build up a diversified industrial and service structure. We have a large pool of skilled manpower and ample entrepreneurial capabilities. There is also a recognition that in many areas of activity, development can best be ensured by freeing them from unnecessary controls and regulations and withdrawing state intervention. At the same time, it is a fact that growth and development of the country cannot be left entirely to the market mechanism. Planning is essential for macro-economic management, for taking care of the poor and the down-trodden, who are mostly outside the market system and have little asset endowment. The challenge is how best to effectively dovetail to them together as complementary to each other. If this is not aimed at democracy in this country may get endangered.

Economic Policy Reforms

The salient features of the New Economic Policy which has come into vogue in 1991 are as follows:

(i) The public sector is to receive backseat and the free market economy is gradually favored.

(ii) Toward this end, a policy of closing down sick public sector industrial units has been announced. The related policy of disinvestment has also been announced.

(iii) More free entry of the private sector in industries.

(iv) Freer entry of foreign capital and investments, including foreign technology transfer.

(v) Freer imports following improvement in foreign exchange reserves situation.

(vi) No upper limit for monopoly business.

(vii) Opening up channels for utilising the 'black money' which was largely the creation or 'Control-permit-raj' into fruitful Investments, and that too, without either explanation or asking any questions.

As an offshoot of some of these measures banks have been permitted to close down branches other than rural areas as well as to swap remunerative branches or those in remote areas.

Comparison of Pre and Post-1991-Economic Reforms

We may get some idea as to how the Indian economy is moving after 1991 Economic reforms. If we look at some indicators which are given below.

1. Rate of Rupee Versus US Dollar Exchange Rate

	Rupees	*US$*
(a) Prior to June 1966.	4.76	1
(b) June 6, 1966 to Mid Dec, 1971	7.50	1

(c)	1971-72	7.44	1
(d)	1990-91	17.95	1
(e)	20th March 2002	45.00	1
2. *Notional Income & Per Capita Income*			
		1993-94	2000-01
(a)	GDP at Current Market Price (Rs. in billions).	8,592	21,800
(b)	GDP at Factor Cost (Constant Price)	5.9%	5.2%
(c)	Per capita GDP (Current Prices)	9,643	Rs. 21,648
(d)	Per Capita GDP (Constant Price)	9,643	Rs.12,782
(e)	Per Capita GDP (Constant Price)	2.6%	5.4%
3. *Prices (Annual Averages)*			
(a)	Wholesale Price Index (% change)	8.1%	7.1%
4. *External Transactions*			
(a)	Exports ($ Millions)	22,213	44, 400
(b)	Imports ... ($ millions)	23,305	49,720
(c)	Balance of ($ millions) Trade.	-1,092	- 5,320
(d)	Foreign Exchange reserves (excluding gold & SD Rs.) ($ millions)	15,068	39,554
(e)	Outstanding external debt ($ Millions)	92,695	100,356
(f)	Debt Service ratio (percent)	25.4%	16.3%

Source: CHIE jen 2002 and Economic Developments in India' A World Bank Country Study. Washington DC (1995).

Summary

Out of the total labourforce in India only a small proportion belongs to the organised sector, which an over-whelming majority is engaged in the unorganised sector. This includes workers engaged in agriculture, forestry, fishing, rural artisans, brick kilns and construction works. The labourers in the unorganised sector of the economy can be distinctly identified into three broad categories (i) Unorganised Urban labourers; (ii) Agricultural labourers, and (iii) Non-agricultural labourers. As per the Census of 1991 these three categories together account for 91% (259 million) of the total work force in the country.

While the organised sector, which comprises of 854 of workforce, is covered by comprehensive social security measures such as medical care, benefits relating to sickness, old age, maternity survival etc., the remaining 92% of the workers (unorganised labour) suffer from various kinds of social insecurity such as illiteracy, food insecurity, uncertainty about employment due to widespread casualisation of work characterised by low earnings, poor working conditions and lack of protection provided by the social security measures.

It is a fact that about one third of our population is still poor,about half of the population is illiterate, many villages do not have access to safe drinking water, productivity of our workforce remains very low in comparison to the international standards. This calls for vigorous efforts on our part. We have to accordingly reorient our strategies and evolve suitable institutions and policies in the wake of the developments.

REFERENCES

1. S.K Sen, *Poverty and Famines: An Essay on Entitlement and Deprivation*, Oxford Claredon Press (1981).
2. S. Chakravorthy, *Development and Famines. The Indian Experience*, Claredon Press Oxford (1987).
3. J. Bhagwati & P. Desai, *Indian Planning for Industrialisation*, Oxford University Press. London (1970).
4. J. Bhagwati & T.N Srinivasan, *India and Economic Reforms*, New Delhi, Ministry of Finance (1993).
5. Tarlok Singh, *Povorty and Social Change*, Orient Longmans: New Delhi (1969).

6. Malcom S. Adisheshaiah (Ed), *Economics of Waste and Development*, and Lancer Press, New Delhi (1989).
7. Gautam Mathur, *Planning for Steady Growth*, Basial Blakwell Delhi (1965).
8. Gautam Mathur, *Economic Justice in a Free Society*, Wiley Eastern Ltd., New Delhi (1994).
9. Gautam Mathur, *Economic Justice in a Free Society*, Wiley Eastern Ltd; New Delhi (1994).
10. Terence J. Byres (Edited), *The State Development Planning and Liberalisation in India*, Oxford University Press, New Delhi (1998).
11. A.K. Sen, *Choice of Techniques*, Basial Blackwell, Oxford (1960).
12. B.R. Virmani & Kala Rao, *Economic Restructuring, Technology Transfer and Human Resource Development*, Response Books, A Division of SAGE Publications, New Delhi (1948).
13. B. Satyanarayan, *"India's Trade with Asia and the Far East Countries*, B.R. Publishing Corporation, New Delhi (1906).
14. B. Satyanaryan, (Edited), *A Comparative Study of Foreign Direct Investment in India and China. Problem and Prospects*, Himalaya Publishing House (1996).
15. B. Satyanaryan, (Edited) *Social Science and Planning for Sustainable Development*, Himalaya Publishing House, (1998).
16. B. Satyanaryan (Edited Jointly), *Essays in Political Economy* Concept Publishing Co. New Delhi (1999).
17. B. Satyanaryan (Edited), *Growth, Industrialisation and New Economic Reforms in India*, Concept Pub. Co. New Delhi (2001).
18. *Economic Survey*, Ca.O.I. 1997-98, 1998-99, 1999-2000 and 2000-2001.

19

World Economic Crisis and Prospects of Its Revival

I am pleased to get this opportunity of addressing this august body of academic experts, policy-makers and other scholars who have assembled for this Seminar. The topic of the Seminar "World Economic Crisis and Prospects of Its Revival" is indeed very pertinent at this stage of World's development for intensive debate and discussions in the present times. I am sure the specialised experts who have assembled here would discuss the various intricate issues that are of relevance to the conceptual and the policy dimensions of the topic. What I intend to do is only to cover a tip of the iceberg as a backdrop to the deliberations of the Seminar.

Introduction

Of the world's 6 billion people, 1.2 billion live on less than $1 a day. About 10 million children under the age of 5 were reported to have died in 1999. More than 113 million primary school age children (majority of them are girls) do not attend any school. More than 4/5 ths of the total world's population are inhabiting in the developing world. The significant question is whether rapid population growth will become a serious problem only to the developing world or will it become a fundamental problem both to rich and poor nations. The statement of Bernard Berelson, Former President of the Population Council "…. the qualities of human lifes prosperity in place of poverty, education in place of ignorance health in place of illness and death, environmental beauty in place of deterioration, full opportunities for the next generations of children in place of current limitations.. …" looks more relevant.

Many knowledgeable people from both rich and poor nations argue that the real problem is not population growth per se but one or all of the following issues. They are as follows:

(a) ***Underdevelopment:*** People argue that underdevelopment is the real problem, and development should be the only goal.

(b) ***World Resource Depletion:*** It is argued that an average North American or European consumer uses up, directly and indirectly, almost sixteen times as much of the food, energy and material resources compared to his counterpart in the third world countries. It is an established fact that high fertility in LDCs is due to their low levels of living, which is again largely the result of the "over-consumption" of the world's scarce resources by rich nations.

(c) ***Population Distribution:*** It is not the absolute numbers, which is causing population problems but their distribution in space. What is needed is to reduce rural - urban migration and a proper spatial distribution of the population in terms of available land and other productive resources.

Deprivations in the Third World: Of the 4.6 billion people in developing countries, more than 850 million are illiterate, nearly a billion lack access to improved water sources, and 2.4 billion lack access to basic sanitation. Nearly 163 million are underweight children under the age of five. This being the case, the rich in this world are becoming more richer. To day, the assets of the world's 358 billionnaries exceed the combined annual incomes of all the countries accounting for nearly half - 45% of the world's people. One would be surprised to note that the Industrialised countries (excluding East Europe and CIS) of the world are having an annual consumption of $16.5 billion (76%) while all the Developing Countries of the world are able to enjoy an annual consumption of only $ 5.2 billion (24%) of the world. This disparity becomes more transparent when one looks at the items of annual expenditure which the world is indulging. All these figures are in US dollars.

1.	Military Spending in the world	$ 780	Billions.
2.	Narcotic drugs in the world	$ 400	"
3.	Alcoholic drinks in Europe	$ 105	"
4.	Cigarette consumption in Europe	$ 50	"
5.	Business Entertainment in Japan	$ 35	"
6.	Bet Poods in Europe & USA	$ 17	"
7.	Perfumes in Europe & USA	$ 12	"
8.	Icecream consumption in Europe	$ 11	"
9.	Cosmetics in USA	$ 8	"
10.	Basic Education for all	$ 6	"
11.	Water & sanitation for all	$ 9	"
12.	Reproductive health for all Women	$ 12	"
13.	Basic health & nutrition	$ 13	"

Source: Human Development Reports (1998).

This only shows the tilted balance which the present World is showing towards items of basic requirements like education, health, nutrition etc. If the expenditure on one item, viz., the military expenditure made by the countries of the World is diverted for some of the basic requirements the World would have been far better. Of course, the actual world scenario is completely different. The picture becomes more glaring if we look at the below mentioned comparative figures:

The ratios of the richest to the poorest are:

(a)	Meat	:	11:1
(b)	Energy	:	17:1
(c)	Overall Consumption	:	16:1
(d)	Fish	:	7:1
(e)	Telephone lines	:	49:1
(f)	Paper	:	77:1
(g)	Cars	:	145::1

TABLE 1

Per Capita Availability in 1995

Sl. No.	*Region*	*Calories per capita per day*	*Teleph-ones per 1000 People*	*Petrol Kg. per capita*	*Cars (1993) per 1000 People*	*Total Energy Kg. of Oil equivalent per capita (1994)*
1	2	3	4	5	6	7
1.	Sub-Saharan Africa	2237	12	27	11	458
2.	Arab States	2903	49	113	42	1215
3.	South Asia	2385	16	10	5	360
4.	East Asia	2717	49	29	6	794
5.	SE Asia & Pacific	2533	29	39	18	619
6.	L. America &	2781	86	152	61	1144
1	2	3	4	5	6	7
I.	All Developing Countries.	2572	39	43	16	670
II.	Industrial	3157	414	500	405	4568

Source: Human Development Report (1998).

All these figures show that divergence between the developed and developing countries, is gradually increasing year after year. The disparities are so enormous. One could as well observe these differences region-wise at the global level for various economic indicators. The table given below records some important items.

It may be observed from Table 1 that the Developing Countries on the whole are having only 39 Telephones (on an average) per 1000 people, while the Developed World is having 414 per 1000 people. Likewise, we can compare other important amenities like per capita petrol consumption. Cars and energy used etc.

I don't like to prolong the discussion at this rate endlessly; I shall try to throw light only on one item which is so important to the humanity as a whole, viz., health, Health expenditure of any country is a fair indicator of the well-being of its people. A wide divergence is discernible between nations in the matter of health expenditure. While the high income group spent more than $ 2500 per capita on health or ten percent of its GDP during 1990-97, the low income countries hardly spent $ 15 per Capita (4.5 of GDP), Just above the estimated $ 12 a year needed to secure the minimum preventive and essential clinical services. For example, the US spent on an average $ 4000 per capita during 1990-97.

Indicators of Development

Ultimately, all developmental activities should raise the standard of living of all citizens of the world. The following table records some important factors like life expectancy, adult literacy, per capita income etc., for various regions of the world.

TABLE 2

Various Indicators of Human Development

Sl. No.	Region	Life expectancy at Birth (1999)	Adult literacy rate (1999) (% Age 15 & above)	Combined Primary, secondary & Tertiary gross enrolement "ratio (%) (1999)	Per capita income (PPP US $) (1999)
I.	Developing Countries	64.5	72.9	61	3,530
(i)	Least developed Countries.	51.7	51.6	38	1,170
(ii)	Arab States.	66.4	61.3	63	4,550
(iii)	East Asia & the Pacific	69.2	85.3	71	3,950
(iv)	L. America & the Caribbean	69.6	87.8	74	6,880
(v)	South Asia.	62.5	55.1	53	2,280
(vi)	Sub-Saharan Africa	48.8	59.6	42	1,640
II.	Eastern Europe and the CIS	68.5	98.6	77	6,290
III.	O E C D	76.6	98.8	87	22,020
IV.	WORLD.	66.7	79.2	65	6,980

Source: "Human Development Report", UNDP, New York (2001).

It may be seen from the foregoing table that the life expectancy and adult literacy rate is hardly in the range of 52% for the least developed countries while it is 78 years and 99% literacy rate as far as the developed countries are concerned. The respective per capita income rates are $ 1170 and $ 22020 for these two regions. These per capita incomes are in PPP terms.

REFERENCES

1. A.K. Sen; *Poverty and Famines: An Essay on Entitlement and Deprivation*, Oxford; Clarendon Press (1981).
2. Malcom S. Adisheshaiah (Ed), *Economics of Waste and Development*, Lancer Press, New Delhi (1889).
3. Anil Markandeya & Julie Richardson (Edited), *Environmental Economics*, Earthscan Publications Ltd., London (1992).

4. Gautam Mathur, *Economic Justice in a Free Society*, Wiley Eastern Ltd., New Delhi (1994),
5. B.R. Virmani & Kala Rao, *Economic Restructuring, Technology Transfer and Human Resource Development*, Response Books, New Delhi (1997).
6. World Bank, *World Development Indicators*, Washington, (USA), 2001.
7. UNDP, *Human Development Report 2001*, New York (2001).
8. B. Satyanarayan (Edited), *A Comparative Steady of Foreign Direct Investment in India and China: Problems and Prospects*, Himalaya Publishing House, Bombay (1996).
9. B. Satyanarayan (Edited), *Social Sciences and Planning for Sustainable Development*, Himalaya Publishing House, Bombay (1998).
10. Bela Balassa, *Trade Prospects for Developing Countries*, Richard D. Irwin, Inc, Illinois (USA) (1964).
11. Bimal Jalan, "Indian Economic Crisis: The Way Ahead" Oxford Univ. Press, New Delhi; (1991).
12. C.T. Kurian, "Global Capitalism and Indian Economy" Orient Longman, New Delhi (1994).

20

Education as an Investment in India*

If one takes the degree of unemployment among the educated Indians as an index, then one is forced to conclude that the education system has over fulfilled its targets in terms of supplying the manpower requirements of the economy. This type of 'saturation', which is apparent, can be cited as one of the many anachronisms thrown up by more than five decades of planning in this country. This is so because of the fact that such a tendency has surfaced when the problem of illiteracy has still extensive proportions. Even when a 'literate' is defined in the most formal terms, as we do, how is it that we have an apparent surplus of educated manpower particularly when a large segment of the economy, viz., the rural segment is virtually manned by illiterate operatives? The purpose of this paper is to investigate the causes leading to the emergence of this phenomenon and suggest remedies.

The causes for this can be better understood if we realise that the education system is neither exgeneously given, nor is superimposed over the rest of the economy. It also cannot be treated as an appendage to the latter. On the other hand, it should be viewed as an integral part of the economy and its role should be rigidly defined in terms of input-output

* Also published in *Convergence Asia*, Vol. 1, No. 4, Oct.-Dec. 2003.

relationship. Thus an investigator taking a micro view of the education system is likely to end up by suggesting solutions to the problems for which the causes lie outside it viz., in the structure of the economic system as a whole. It is in such a case that one comes across a series of partial solutions like suggesting a halt to the expansion of the education sector, selective intake into the system, expansion of lower tier at the expense of higher tier etc. These adhoc solutions arising out of taking a blinkered view of the situation, besides having no inherent curative-value, actually inflict damage on the system.

The proper way of evaluating the benefits following from the education system is to consider its role in the process of economic development. This then is the primary criterion for evaluation. A system which is pro-development is rated highly while the one which impedes it is rated at a correspondingly lower level. Thus, the mode of evaluation itself acquires a functional bias and varies according to the overall economic and social benefits which are the ultimate resultants of the system. In short, it has to be viewed in the context of the strategy of development which is the optimum for a country at that point of time.

The strategy of economic development that is being followed presently is so inappropriate to the endowments we have that it has ultimately resulted in the emergence of what is appropriately called by late Professor Gautam Mathur as the "Glass Curtain Economy". Here the accent in the organised industrial sector is on the production of consumer luxuries and semi-luxuries with the help of techniques which are being imported (or imitated) from advanced countries, are so sophisticated that they render themselves as inappropriate to the large population with their limited assets and incomes. The degree of sophistication which these industries (called the H-Sector, for short) output used for the production of these types of equipments. Such H-using techniques are generally labour - saving and capital -Intensive in nature. Highly capital - intensive techniques, when adopted in our environs tend to save the factor whose supply is abundant thus indicating the irrelevance of such techniques to us

Further, adoption of these techniques results in an erosion of the growth potential of the H-Sector through Constant draining of its physical resources. When the technology adopted demands huge proportion of H-output as necessary input, the rate of growth of H-Sector is retarded thus converting itself into a bottleneck to the overall growth of the economy Hence, highly capital - intensive techniques besides causing a low growth rate, causes the denial of employment opportunities to the millions of aspirants in the economy.

Such an economy leads to the emergence of two distinct classes who symbolise glaring and seemingly irrevocable differences when juxtaposed. We then have an atomistic minority of the population having a very high standard of living (since the whole organised industrial sector caters to their needs by producing a collection of luxury goods which they conveniently brand as 'functional necessities" coexisting with a large mass of people for whom the access to such a living is permanently denied in this system. The economy is thus vivisected by 'Glass Curtain' on either side of which exist these two classes with disparities so huge that the massive majority which is outside it can only stand there and stare. This therefore is a system which denies Growth and Social Justice.

It is then no wonder that the education system corresponding to this also exhibits gross futility as to its purpose. The system as it obtains today with its emphasis on liberal and formal education is capable of producing prototypes whose place in the development scheme is hard to define.

The majority of the 'educated' (as they are called in this system) are unsuitable for manning the sophisticated technique used in the economy without an expensive in-service training which then makes the original effort redundant. The liberal bias in the syllabi makes them unsuitable for functional occupations and thus, a large segment of the economy comprising the agricultural and Agri - industrial sectors wanting operatives of the functional type is starved of such personnel.

The result is that these people tend to apply to the organised industrial sector for sustenance. They are denied this because of the inability of the industrial sector to absorb them on account of the reasons mentioned above Thus, we have the phenomenon of 'educated', unemployment even when we are at the fringe of the problem of illiteracy.

When such an educated man power is priced on the basis of their contribution to the economic system, the aggregate value comes out to be much lower than the book value accounted for them. Thus, when one evaluates the returns on Investment in education sector on the basis of such prices, the resultant rate of return will be much lower than one obtained by computing it along the conventional cost - benefit lines. It is the former parameter which ought to be used for considering the amount of subsidy to the educational sector.

A low rate of return (on the basis of shadow valuation) indicates that the education sector, as it obtains today, is unsuited to the social and economic requirements and thus expenditure on it is not only anti -developmental, but also inflationary. Advocates of higher financial subvention to this sector to augment their chosen tiers should realise that their plea for higher allotment for this sector reinforces inflationary processes Another source of such reinforcement is the fact that there is a very high incidence of wastage during the movement of pupils along various tiers of the system. The Department of Economics, Osmania University has calculated that out of every 10,000 pupils entering the system at the primary level, only 16 come out as Post -graduates.

REFERENCES

1. Anderson, A & Bowman, M.J. (Ed) (1965): *Education and Economic Development*, London: Cass & Co. Ltd.
2. Ansari, M.M. (1997), *Cost Effectiveness of Higher Education. A Critical Assessment*, New Delhi, Concept Publishing Co.
3. Association of Indian Universities (1975), *Higher Education & Development*, New Delhi, AIU.
4. Azad, J.L (1975), *Financing of Higher Education in India*, New Delhi, Sterling Publishers.
5. Azad, J.L. (1988), *Higher Education India: The Deepening Financial Crisis*, New Delhi, Radiant Publishers.
6. Benson, C (1963), *Perspectives on the Economics of Education*, Boston, Honghton, Mifflin.
7. Blaag, M (1969-Ed), *Economics of Education*, (Vol. 1 & 2) Penguin Modern Economics Readings: Harmonds with Penguin.
8. Blaag, M (1970), *An Introduction to the Economics of Education*, London, Penguin Books Ltd.
9. Brahmanand, PR (1967), "Economic Theory and Investment in Education" in *Education as Investment*, Meerut, Meenakshi Prakasham.
10. Chauhan, CPS (1990), *Higher Education in India: Achievements, Failures and Strategies*, New Delhi, Ashish Pub House.
11. Chitnis, Suma & Philip G. Albach. (Ed) (1993) *Higher Education Reform in India: Experience and Perspectives*, New Delhi'. Sage Publications.
12. Conn, E (1975), *Economics of Education*, London, Balimger Publishing Co.
13. Hams, S.E. (1962), *Higher Education: Resources and Finances*, New York, McGraw Hill Book Co.
14. Hedge Dodeyar (1992) *Economics of Education; A Study of Indian Experience*, New Delhi, Himalaya Publishing House.

21

Measuring Poverty Levels with Reference to India*

The measurement of poverty is a difficult job. At the extreme, those who go hungry every day, do not have adequate clothes and sleep on the payement are clearly poor. But families which do not suffer from malnutrition and yet cannot afford to buy medicines when illness strikes will also, rightfully, consider themselves poor.

The most common measure of poverty is one which counts the number of people who do not earn enough to buy food that gives the bare minimum required for sustenance. There are many variants of this "income" measure of poverty. Now a new measure of poverty has been developed. This is know as "Capability Poverty Measure" (CPM) that has been put together for a number of countries in the 1996 edition of the UNDP's Human Development Report (HRD). The CPM is broadly the proportion of the population that suffers from malnutrition, is illiterate and experiences risks in reproduction.

The very basic human capabilities would then be the freedom from under-nourishment, from available infant morality, from high morbidity and also the freedom to be

* Reprint from BN Singh et al., (ed.), *Economic Reforms in India*, 2003.

educated and live long. (Higher income in this perception of development is not an end in itself but merely one of the means to acquire the necessary capabilities).

The CPM is an index comprising three indicators:

The first indicator is the percentage of children under five who are underweight. This measures the deprivation in nourishment. The second indicator is the proportion of births unattended by trained personal. This measures the lack of capability for healthy reproduction. And the third indicator is the percentage of women over 15 who are illiterate. This measures the deprivation in education. The CPM is the average of these three indicators. The 1996 edition of the HRD has estimated the CPM for 101 developing countries. Table 1 present the CPM and the underlying statistics for *a* select group of countries. It becomes evident that the Asian countries other than Sri Lanka have very high CPM values because on all three counts - nutrition, literacy and healthy reproduction - they do badly. A low per capita income is not an obstacle to improving the three capabilities.

On the whole, the HRD estimates that 37 per cent of the people in developing countries are capability poor while by the income criterion, the figure is only 21 per cent. One question is how the CPM compares with the Human Development Index (HDI), also pioneered and estimated by the UNDP in the annual HDI. (The HDI for each country is a composite measure of life expectancy, education and percapita income). There are differenoes between the two indices.

It may be seen from Table 1 that the Capability Poverty Measure is as low as 3 per cent for Chile, 17.5 per cent for China, while it is as high as 80 per cent for Bangladesh and nearly 62 per cent for India. In the same manner, the percentage of births unattended by the trained health personnel is as high as 90 per cent for Bangladesh, 65 per cent and 67 per cent for Pakistan and India respectively. The underweight children under the age of five is also very high for Bangladesh (66%) and India (53%). Likewise, the percentage of Female illiteracy is as high as 77 per cent for Pakistan, 75 per cent for Bangladesh and 64 per cent for India. This is as low as 4 per cent for South Korea and 5.5 per cent for Chile. This shows that the variation of these indicator is wide which more or less depends upon a country's overall economic development.

TABLE 1

Capability Poverty Measures for some Select Countries

Sl. No.	*Country*	*CPM Value*	*Births unattended by trained health per sonal (%) 1983-1994*	*Underweight children under age five (%) 1985-95*	*Female illite-racy rate (%) 1993*
1.	Chile	2.8	2	1	5.5
2.	South Korea	8.6	11	11	3.9
3.	China	17.5	6	17	29.1
4.	Sri Lanka	19.3	6	38	13.8
5.	south Africa	30.4	29	43	19.2
6.	Indonesia	42.3	64	40	23.1
7.	Pakistan	60.8	65	40	77.0
8.	India	61.5	67	53	64.0
9.	Bangladesh	76.9	90	66	75.0

Source: Human Development Report (1996).

Table 2 Records statics representing both type viz., CPM and Income Poverty Levels of some countries.

It may be observed from the foregoing table that the Capability Poverty Measure for Bangladesh is about 77 per cent, while the proportion of people below the Poverty Line is 47.5 per cent. The respective proportions for India are: 61.5 per cent and 25.4 per cent. The difference could be observed for all the remaining countries.

TABLE 2

Capability Poverty and Income Poverty

(Per cent)

Sl. No.	*Country*	*People who are Capability Poor (CPM) 1993*	*People who are income Poor (Head Count Index)*
1.	Bangladesh	76,9	47.5
2.	India	61.5	25.4
3.	Pakistan	60.8	34.0
4.	Indonesia	42.3	16.7
5.	Ghana	39.3	35.9
6.	Zimbabwe	22.3	25.5
7.	Sri Lanka	19.3	22.4
8.	China	17.5	10.9
9.	Venezuela	15.2	31.3

Source: HRD (1996).

Table 3 gives an idea about India's Rural and Urban Poverty break-up ratio.

TABLE 3

India's Head-Count Poverty Ratio

Year	*Rural*	*Urban*	*Combined*
1983*	45.65	40.79	44.48
1987-88*	39.09	38.20	38.86
1989-90	33.70	36.00	34.28
1990-91	35.04	35.29	35.11
1992	41.70	37.80	40.70
1993-94*	37.27	32.36	35.07
1994-95	38.03	34.24	36.08
1995-96	38.29	30.05	36.08
1997*	38.46	33.97	37.23

Note: *Denotes large sample surveys.

Source: NSS data used bv S.P. Gupta (1999).

It may be seen that the proportion of Indian population below the poverty line was about 45 per cent (rural and urban put together) during eighties while it has come down to around 35 per cent during nineties.

22

Trends in Trading Patterns of Asia-Pacific

Asia Pacific includes the below mentioned groups and countries: (1) Japan, (2) The Newly Industrialised Countries (NICS)—Hong Kong, Korea, Singapore and Taiwan; (3) ASEAN, (4) Indonesia, Malaysia, Philippines, Thailand; and (4) People's. Republic of China. Asia-Pacific region is twice as large as Europe and USA. The changing pattern of production, trade and investment in accordance with the changing comparative advantage in the region has seen one tier of countries fuelling the economies of another tier, thereby resulting in deeper integration. Japan is the epicentre of the region. The next stage, where the manufacturing activity was relocated was the NICs—Hong Kong, Korea, Singapore and Taiwan. Next came the ASEAN (4)-Indonesia, Malaysia, Philippines and Thailand and then China. These diverse and expanding production, trade and investment linkages have been important ingredients in the growth of the Asia-Pacific as a dynamic region. Asia-Pacific, now the driving force of the global economy must have vision of what its role in the new global order should be, so that it is realised in the years to come.

Most of the Asia Pacific countries have chosen an exported

growth model and therefore trade has an important role to play in each of the country's economic development processes. Besides, the trade amongst these countries has also been significant and has prompted the development of the region as a whole. Therefore, an in-depth analysis of the trading patterns in the region would help us to understand the growth pattern in the region. It would also give us an insight into the 'economic relationship between countries in the region and the scope for a more proactive region trading arrangement

Asia-Pacific Total Trade

The spectacular growth of Asia Pacific region during the last two decades has been the focus of global attention and admiration Because of this growth, the region had achieved such economic resilience that, in spite of the slowing down in global economic output in some years, it had continued to maintain a remarkable rate of economic growth, almost twice as high as the global average In fact it was expected that the dynamism of Asia-Pacific was to provide a stimulus to the growth of the world economy The increasingly open market and big emerging economies such as China, India and Indonesia, are arousing the interest of the world business community has the markets of the future for trade and investment. The East-Asian crisis of 1997 and its spectacular recovery have added another dimension to the already increasing interest in the region. Developing economies are looking towards East Asia for several lessons to be learnt so as to emulate the 'miracle' and avoid the 'crisis'. It is in this context, a review of the growth trends in trade of Asia Pacific countries is undertaken. This paper analyses three main aspects of Asia Pacific total trade:

- Asia Pacific trade and share in World trade
- Country/group-wise share in Asia Pacific
- Asia Pacific trade by broad regions.

(i) Asia Pacific Trade and Share in World Trade

The merchandise trade of Asia Pacific (the ten economies together)increased more than four times from an average annual of US$ 608 billion between 1980-84 to US$ 2568 billion between 1995-99. This phenomenal growth in the region's external trade, far above the world average, has resulted in the region's rising 24% during 1995/2000 (Table-1). While Asia Pacific trade experienced an average annual growth of 11% between 1985-89 over the 1980-84 periods, the growth was still higher at 16.5% between 1990-94 over the 1985-89 period A look at Table-2 shows that growth rates in both these periods are much higher than the average World growth in trade In spite of the East Asian crisis in 1997, the growth rates in 1995-99 over the 1990-94 periods are also slightly higher than the growth rates in world trade. It is noteworthy that the legion's developing economies have achieved much higher growth than the Asia Pacific average The lour NICs have achieved the fastest rales of growth in the 1980s and have maintained the momentum in the 1990s Among the ASEAN-4, Malaysia and Thailand have witnessed high growth rales, while the performance of Indonesia and Philippines has been relatively sluggish China has been the star performer of Asia Pacific with its exports glowing nearly twelve times in this period. All countries showed fall in trade in 1998 and negative growth due to the adverse impact of the 1997 economic crisis in East Asia.

Looking at the country shares in world trade we see that trade, although Japan's share in world trade has declined from an annual average of nearly 8% between 1980-84 to 6.8% in 1995-99, yet it Continues to be the leader in Asia with the largest individual share. Its share in world exports has fallen from a high of 9.5% in 1985-89 to 7.7 in 1980-84 to 6% in 1994-99. After the Plaza accord in September 1985, the value of the Yen began to rise rapidly, adversely affecting those sectors of the manufacturing heavily dependent on exports Fluctuations in the exchange rate of yen have had a major impact on Japanese trade performance and on corporate balance sheets with large trade component. In 1997, export (merchandise) volume rose 9.5% but the dollar value of merchandise exports rose only 2.5% due to fall in the value of yen. In 1998, export volume is estimated to have risen by 4.5% but the dollar value is estimated to have declined. In the same year import volume has risen only modestly but imports in value terms have declined significantly. In 1999 a needed impetus for the recovery of the economies hit by the crisis in Asia, but the yen's appreciation against the dollar significantly eroded such export competitiveness. In 2000, as most of the crisis hit economies are showing sharp signs of upswing. Japan's total trade has grown rapidly by 17.6% with growing demand from these Asian Countries. Its share in world trade now is between 7-8%.

The NICs have shown an upward trend in their share in world trade, both as a group as well as individually. The NICs share in world merchandise trade has doubled from an average of 5% in 1980-84 to 10% between 1995-99. Both, the share of exports and imports in world exports and imports have also doubled from 5% to 10% in that period. In 1998, however there has been a slight decline in NICs share in world trade to 8.2% due to the negative growth in trade but the 1999/2000 trade figures show positive growth in trade and the gradually increasing share in world trade, thereby implying that the countries have recovered from crises.

The growth trends in trade have been phenomenal between 1980 and almost up to 1995. The NICs total trade experienced an average annual growth rate of 16.3% between 1980-84 and 1985-89,21% between 1985-89,21% between 1985-89 and 1990-94 and 11% between 1990-94 and 1995-99. Most of the initial growth from 1980 onwards is mainly due to the NICs becoming the platform for the Japanese manufacturing industries. While Japan found it no longer profitable to carry on production in labour intensive manufacturing due to Rising labour costs and low value addition and moved to high technology and products with greater value addition, most of the low technology., labour intensive manufacturing shifted location to the NICs where labour and raw materials were cheaper This resulted in the spurt of trading and investment activities in the region and especially between Japan and NICs.

While Japan pumped in vestment to set up manufacturing bases in the NICs, the NICs in turn exported low-end parts, components and labour intensive products from these manufacturing bases, back to Japan to feed their high-technology industries. This resulted in the rising foreign trade of the NICs, not only interregional but also as a part of world trade. It helped the NICs get the required investment and know how for setting up the manufacturing infrastructure and developing the NICs block. In 1998, the growth in foreign trade has been negative for Asia Pacific. (World trade also experienced a slight slump in 1998) This is due to the adverse impact of the East-Asian crisis that hit most of the countries in the region. In fact all countries in the region experienced a negative growth trend in trade in 1998 because the Asia-Pacific economies have strong backward and forward linkages and a trickle down effect is inevitable. From 1999, positive growth trends show sure signs of recovery. Individually in the NICs, all countries show a slight, more or less doubling of share in world trade between 1980 and 1999. Only Hong Kong's share has nearly tripled from an average annual of 1.2% om 1980-84 to 3.4% in 1995-99.

The next group, the ASEAN region is rich in resource but low in technology. The ASEAN region has also had a similar experience as the NICs with most countries following the flying geese model. With rising costs of labour and material in the NICs, the manufacturing locations have now moved to the ASEAN countries, Besides possessing cheap labour, they are also rich in natural resources. Japan and the NICs have funded many projects in the region for resource extraction and labour intensive manufacturing. Most of the textile and other low technology manufacturing bases are now relocated in ASEAN countries. Infrastructural investment in oil extraction, road and transportation etc., have resulted in the flow of investment into the region and helped in expanding the trade in the region. The ASEAN-4, i.e., Indonesia, Malaysia, Philippines and Thailand together show an increase in world trade from an average annual of 2.4% in 1980-84 to 4% in 1995-99. Individually also their shares in world trade seems to have doubled between 1980 and 1997 (except Indonesia). While Indonesia's share in world trade has remained around 1 %. Malaysia's share has doubled from 0.73% to 1.4%,Philipines from 0.3% to 0.6%, while Thailand's share increased from 0.5% to 1.1% the ASEAN region was most badly hit by the Asian crisis. While all the countries showed high growth rate in trade between 1985-95, there has been a sharp decline in trade growth in 1996-and 1997 (except for Philippines). For one, the competition from China where costs are still lower, has posed an obstacle in ASEAN's expanding foreign trade Second, the global trade reversionary trend seems to have started showing up right from mid 1996. All growth rates in trade showed negative trend in 1998, the ASEAN region being the worst hit. In 1999, however signs of recovery were being felt with positive growth in trade in Malaysia and Thailand and a fall in the negative trend in Indonesia and Philippines.

China the sleeping tiger seems to have awakened with its share in world trade tripling from an average annual of

1% in 1980-84 to around 3% in 1995-99. China seems to have tapped a high share of the low technology, labour intensive manufacturing in the region and is posing a major threat to the ASEAN foreign trade. China has the advantage of low labour costs, a controlled and planned production system, and an all-pervading Confucius environment, all of which together have resulted in the expanding production and foreign trade It's trade within the Asia-Pacific region and outside with USA and EU is steadily expanding, China is being perceived as the next giant of the region. Although the Asian crisis did effect China but it was minimal with a slight negative growth of less than 1% In 1999 growth in trade has picked up to 10%.

Overall the Asia-Pacific share in world trade has grown from an average annual of 16% in 1980- 84 to 24% in 1995-99. This increase in total trade is experienced both in exports and imports of goods where exports increased from 16% to 26% while imports increased from 15% to 22%. Although the growth trends in trade have been influenced with the world-trading environment, yet the region has reached a stage where it can easily overcome the global fluctuations in trade. The financial crisis of 1997 that hit the Asian economies has caused a temporary downswing in the economic activity of the region, but recent trends show that the countries are on the recovery path.

(ii) Country/Group-wise Share in Asia Pacific

Table-3 gives us a picture of country/group-wise shares in the total trade of Asia Pacific region. Japan, as is obvious, has the highest share in Asia Pacific trade, but the share seems to be gradually falling. While in 1980-84 Japan's trade on an average constituted 47% of the region's trade, its share has fallen to 29% during 1995-99 This is because although Japan's trade has fallen due to the increasing shares of the other three entities, i.e., the NICs, the ASEAN-4 and China. As was seen in the earlier section, the rapid growth in trade in the NICs, ASEAN-4 and China has lead to the spectacular increase in the relative shares of these countries/groups not only in the Asia Pacific trade but also in world trade.

The NICs group share in Asia-Pacific trade has gone up from an average annual of 31% in 1980- 84 to 42% in 1995-2000. The NICs initially formed the production base for Japanese lowed technology inputs and components but are now themselves the producers of high technology products, including sophisticated machinery and equipment. Among the NICs; Hong Kong is the largest contributor to Asia Pacific trade, with its share increasing from 7.7% in 1980-84, has increased to 10% of total Asia-Pacific trade in 1995-99. Taiwan's share in Asia-Pacific total trade has risen from 7% in 1980-84 to 9% in 1995-99

The next group ASEAN-4 still seems to have a relatively small share in Asia Pacific trade, though it has a large potential. The relocation of production and outsourcing of parts, components and intermediate products in the ASEAN by major companies, especially from Japan has contributed phenomenally to the growth and diversification of manufactured exports from these countries. For instance intra-firm trade plays a significant role in the manufactured exports from these countries. For instance intra-firm trade plays a significant role in the manufactured exports of Malaysia and Thailand. In ASEAN-4, Malaysia has the highest share (5.8) followed by Thailand (4.2) in the Asia-Pacific trade in 2000. Indonesia's share has fallen from 5.8% in 1980 to 2.8% in 2000, while Philippines share has remained the same (2.5%).

The growing integration of China in the global market place is evident from its trade exposure during the 1980s measured by the share of its trade in GDP. For China, its trade exposure has increased three times from 12% in 1980 to 36% in 2000. China's integration with the Asia- Pacific can be seen by its share in the total Asia trade, which has nearly doubled from around 7% in 1980 to 13% in 1994-99 and further to 15% in 2000.

The Asia-Pacific region has not only shown dynamism in world trade, but has also achieved significant and sustained growth in intra-regional trade. While the Asia-Pacific intra-regional trade will be discussed in the latter section, it would be worthwhile to see the broad regional distribution of Asia-Pacific trade to know its main partner countries/groups in world trade. The next section shows the direction of Asia-Pacific trade by broad regions and share of both inter and intra-regional trade.

(iii) Asia Pacific Trade by Broad Regions

The Asia Pacific trade with the rest of the world still constitutes 50-55% of their total world trade. The broad breakdown of the regional destination of merchandise trade of Asia Pacific is given in Table-4 While intra-regional trade was only 31% in 1980 and extra regional trade was as high as 69%,' this share has increased with intra-regional trade constituting 41% in 1990 and nearly 49% in 2000. Extra-regional trade on the other hand has declined from 69% in 1980 to 51% in 2000. In the pattern of intra-regional trade, North America (N.A.) and Western Europe (W.E.) constitute the predominant markets for the exports of almost all the economies of the region For many countries of the region, the USA is the single largest trading partner For the region as a whole, North America (of which USA is the main trading country) absorbed nearly 24% of its exports in 1980,29% in 1990 and 26% in 2000. Similarly, Western Europe (of which European Union is the major block) accounted 16% of the region's exports in 1980, 19% in 1990 and a decline back to 16% in the post-crisis period in 2000. More importantly, the United States and the European Union are the main markets for the manufactured exports of Asia Pacific countries, both for the high technology products of Japan and the NICs and for the labour-intensive manufacturers of the ASEAN and China As for imports, the share of North America has declined from 20% to 16% while that of Western Europe has marginally increased from 10% to 12% in the period. Overall there is not much change in the total trade shares of North America which constituted 22% of total Asia Pacific trade in 1980, went up to 25% in 1990 and declined to 22% in 2000. Similarly, the region's trade with Western Europe was 14% in 1980 increased to 17% in 1990 and declined to 14% in 2000.

The shares of the other regions are relatively small with Latin America having a share of 3% and Africa's share declining from 3% in 1980 to 1.3% in 2000. All other regions/countries(for eg.Eastern Europe, Middle East, Oceania etc) together constituted 28% of Asia Pacific trade in 1980, but this share has declined to 11% in 2000. This clearly shows that North America dominated by US and Western Europe mainly European Union, continue to remain important as trading partners for Asia Pacific while the trade with other regions seems' to have declined. Therefore, the share of overall extra-regional or inter-regional trade has declined in the total trade of Asia Pacific, while the share of intra-regional trade has increased.

Although the markets of the Asia Pacific countries have grown in importance, thereby enhancing intra-regional trade, the markets of North America and Western Europe continue to remain vital for exports of Asia Pacific countries In fact, Asia Pacific gets a major part of its dynamism due to its trade with these two regions Therefore the promotion of intra-regional trade must be consistent with and complementary to enhancing the securing access to the markets of mainly US and European Union. In other words, intra-regional and inter-regional trade will have to go hand in hand to maintain the momentum and growth of Asia Pacific's external trade.

TABLE 1

Asia-Pacific Trade and Share in World Trade

(a= Average annual; Fig. In US$ million; percentage)

	1980-1984	*1985-1989*	*1990-1994*	*1995-1999*	*2000*
I. Japan					
Total	283137(7)	39300()(8)	584125(8)	739714(7)	858760(7)
Exports	147475(8)	231759(10)	340034(9)	416500(8)	479249(8)
Imports	135662(7)	161240(6)	244091(6)	323214(6)	379511(6)
II. NICs					
Total	189123(5)	343555(7)	698575(9)	1089321(10)	1308166(10)
Exports	90854(5)	178577(7)	345387(9)	542852(10)	660324(10)
Imports	98269(3)	164978(7)	353187(9)	'546469(10)	647842(10)
(i) Hong Kong					
Total	47173(1)	99992(2)	238641(3)	368345(3)	414665(3)
Exports	22538(1)	50078(2)	117330(3)	176016(3)	201860(3)
Imports	24635(1)	49915(2)	121310(3)	192330(3)	212805(3)
(ii) Korea					
Total	48761(1)	89879(2)	162115(2)	259262(2)	332749(3)
Exports	22860(1)	46711(2)	78262(2)	132198(2)	172268(3)
Imports	25900(1)	43168(2)	83852(2)	127064(2)	160481(2)
(iii) Singapore					
Total	48734(1)	67207(1)	146845(2)	238906(2)	272420(2)
Exports	21414(1)	31619(1)	69360(1)	118645(2)	137875(2)
Imports	27320(1)	35588(1)	77485(2)	120261(2)	134545(2)
(iv) Taiwan					
Total	44454(1)	86476(2)	150974(2)	222809(2)	288332(2)
Exports	24041(1)	50169(2)	80435(2)	115994(2)	148321(2)
Imports	20413(1)	36307(1)	70539(2)	106815(2)	140011(2)

III ASEAN- 4					
Total	92457(2)	106422(2)	246198(3)	417041(4)	472189(4)
Exports	48214(3)	35779(2)	118609(3)	211835(4)	263296(4)
Imports	44242(2)	50643(2)	127589(3)	205207(4)	208893(3)
(i) Indonesia					
Total	92457(1)	106422(1)	246198(1)	417041(1)	472189(1)
Exports	21906(1)	18378(1)	32777(1)	51345(1)	56321(1)
Imports	14240(1)	12761(1)	26759(1)	37060(1)	30962(0.5)
(ii) Malaysia					
Total	25915(1)	33690(1)	84286(1)	149769(1)	180334(1.5)
Exports	13494(1)	18693(1)	42082(1)	77748(1)	98135(2)
Imports	12422(1)	14997(1)	42203(1)	72022(1)	82199(1)
(iii) Philippines					
Total	13193(0.3)	13447(0.3)	26443(0.4)	61355(0.8)	73591(0.8)
Exports	5361(0.3)	5981(0.2)	10309(0.3)	25909(0.5)	39783(1)
Imports	7832(0.4)	7466(0.3)	16134(0.4)	35447(1)	33808(0.5)
(iv) Thailand					
Total	17203(0.5)	28146(0.8)	75933(1)	117512(1)	130981(1)
Exports	7454(0.4)	12727(0.5)	33441(1)	56834(1)	69057(1)
Imports	9749(0.5)	15419(1)	42492(1)	60678(1)	61924(1)
IV. China					
Total	43144(1)	88436(2)	170739(2)	322301(3)	455429(4)
Exports	21680(1)	39747(2)	86873(2)	176778(3)	249297(4)
Imports	21464(1)	48688(2)	83866(2)	145523(3)	206132(3)
Asia Pacific					
Total	607861(16)	931412(19)	1699636(22)	2568377(24)	3094544(24)
Exports	308223(17)	505863(21)	890903(24)	1347965(25)	1652166(26)
Imports	299638(16)	425549(17)	808733(21)	1220412(22)	1442378(22)
World Trade					
Total	3793300	4959400	7598200	10923800	12822900
Exports	1863400	2436100	3754800	5410700	6310100
Imports	1929900	2523400	3843400	5513100	6512800

TABLE 2

Growth Trends in Asia-Pacific Total Trade

(average annual growth)

Countries	*1985-89/1980-84*	*1990-94/1985-89*	*1995-99/1990-94*
I. JAPAN	7.6	9.7	5.4
II. NICs	16.3	20.6	11.2
III. ASEAN-4	3.0	26.2	13.8
IV. CHINA	21.0	18.6	17.7
ASIA PACIFIC	11.2	16.5	10.2
WORLD TRADE	6.2	10.6	8.7

TABLE 3

Country Share in Asia Pacific Trade

(Percentage)

		1980-1984	*1985-1989*	*1990-1994*	*1995-1999*	*2000*
I.	Japan					
	Total	47	42	34	29	28
	Exports	48	46	38	31	29
	Imports	45	38	30	26	26
II.	NICs					
	Total	31	37	41	42	42
	Exports	29	35	39	40	40
	Imports	33	39	44	45	45
(i)	Hong Kong					
	Total	8	11	14	14	13
	Exports	7	10	13	13	12
	Imports	8	12	15	16	15
(ii)	Korea					
	Total	8	10	10	10	11
	Exports	7	9	9	10	10
	Imports	9	10	10	10	11

(iii)	Singapor					
	Total	8	7	9	9	9
	Exports	7	6	8	9	8
	Imports	9	8	10	10	9
(iv)	Taiwan					
	Total	7	9	9	9	9
	Exports	8	10	9	9	9
	Imports	7	9	9	9	10
III.	ASEAN-4					
	Total	15	11	14	16	15
	Exports	16	11	13	16	16
	Imports	15	12	16	17	14
(i)	Indonesia					
	Total	6	3	4 1 3	3	
	Exports	7	4	4	4	3
	Imports	5	3	3	3	2
(ii)	Malaysia					
	Total	4	4	5	6	6
	Exports	4	4	5	6	6
	Imports	4	4	5	6	6
(iii)	Philippines					
	Total	2	1	2	2	2
	Exports	2	1	1	2	2
	Imports	3	2	2	3	2
(iv)	Thailand					
	Total	3	3	4	5	4
	Exports	2	3	4	4	4
	Imports	3	4	5	5	4
IV.	China					
	Total	7	9	10	13	15
	Exports	7	8	10	13	15
	Imports	7	11	10	12	14

TABLE 4

Asia Pacific Trade By Broad Regions

PART-I

Regions	*1980*		
	Exp	*Imp*	*Total*
North America	63270 (24.3)	54575 (20.4)	114696 (21.7)
Western Europe	42248 (16.2)	28633 (10.4)	71454 (13.5)
Latin America	5963 (2.3)	5423 (2.0)	11386 (2.2)
Africa	11656 (4.5)	5825 (2.2)	17481 (3.3)
Others	56304 (21.7)	92050 (34.3)	150930 (28.6)
Extra-Regional Trade	179441 (69.0)	186506 (69.6)	365947 (69.3)
Intra-Regional Trade	80563 (31.0)	81598 (30.4)	162161 (30.7)
Total Asia-Pacific Trade	260004	268104	52X108

Part-II

Regions	*1990*	*2000*				
	Exp	Imp	Total	Exp	Imp	Total
North America	185986 (29.12)	123922 (21.0)	309908 (25.8)	402687 (26.8)	208772 (16.0)	611459 (21.8)
Western Europe	118555 (18.56)	94246 (15.9)	2128801 (17.3)	235199 (15.5)	164409 (12.6)	399608 (14.2)
Latin America	4692 (0.73)	12352 (2.1)	17044 (1.4)	16323 (1.1)	67531 (5.2)	83854 (3.0)
Africa	11920 (1.87)	6614 (1.1)	18534 (1.5)	20023 (1.3)	16720 (1.3)	36743 (1.3)
Others	64208 (10.05)	97957 (16.6)	162165 (13.2)	147588 (9.8)	157615 (12.1)	305203 (10.9)

Extra-Regional Trade	385361 (60.00)	335091 (56.7)	720452 (58.6)	821820 (54.6)	615047 (47.2)	1436867 (51.2)
Intra-Regional Trade	253180 (40.00)	255871 (43.3)	509051 (41.4)	682025 (45.4)	687320 (52.8)	1369345 (48.8)
Total Asia-Pacific Trade	638541	590962	1229503	1503845	1302367	2806212

REFERENCES

1. John Naisbitt: (1996), *Megatrends Asia*, Simon & Schuster, Rockefeller Centre, New York.
2. John Naisbitt & Patricia Aburdence (1991), *Megatrends*-2000, Simon & Schuster, New York.
3. MR. Agarwal (1979), *Regional Economic Cooperation in South-Asia*, Sultan Chand & Co., New Delhi.
4. David Aikman (1986), *Pacific Rim: Area of Changes, Area of Opportunities*, Little Brown & Co., Boston.
5. Asian Development Bank (1997), *Emerging Asia*, ADB Publication.
6. Colin Bradford (Ed) (1987), *Trade and Structural Change in Pacific Asia*, UCP, Chicago.
7. K. Dilip Das (1996), *The Asia-Pacific Economy*, Macmillan Press Ltd., New Delhi.
8. Peter Drysdale (1988), *International Economic Pluralism: Policy in East Asia and the Pacific*, Allen & Unwin, Sydney.
9. IIFT, (1995), *Studies in Trade and Investment: Review and Analysis of Intra- regional Trade Flows in Asia and the Pacific*, New Delhi.
10. V.R. Panchamukhi (1989), *Growth, Trade and Structural Change in the Asian region*, RIS, New Delhi.
11. V.R. Panchamukhi and Rehman Sobhan (Ed) (1955), *Towards an Asian Economic Area*, RIS, New Delhi.
12. Gautam Mathur, (1965), *Planning for Steady Growth*, Basil Blockwell. Oxford.
13. B. Satyanarayan, (1986), *India's Trade with Asia and the Far East Countries*, B.R. Publishing Corporation, New Delhi.
14. B. Satyanarayan (Ed) (1996), *A Comparative Study of Foreign Direct Investment in India and China: Problems and Prospects*, HPH, Bombay.

23

Role of Small Scale and Agro-Based Industries in India in the Context of Liberalisation Policy

Introduction

Industrialisation has a major role to play in economic development of the developing countries like India. The gap in per capita incomes between developed and developing countries is largely reflected in the structure of their economies. The former are largely industrial economies, while the latter are predominantly agriculture-oriented. The Table 1 shows the positive relationship between per capita income and the share of manufacturing output.

Historically, industrial development has proceeded through three stages. In the first stage, industries are concerned with the processing or primary products. The second stage comprises of the transformation of materials into manufactured products. The third stage, consists of the manufacture of machines and other capital equipments.

Growth of Small Scale Industries (SSIs) in India

A significant feature of the Indian economy since Independence is the rapid growth of small scale industrial sector. In the Industrial Policy Resolutions (IPRs of 1948 & 1956) the

TABLE 1

Industrial Distribution of Gross Domestic Product and Per Capita Income (2000)

Sl. No.	*Country*	*Per capita Income in US dollars (2000)*	*Origin of Domestic factor cost Percentages)*		
			Agriculture	*Indus-try*	*Services*
1	2	3	4	5	6
1.	U.S.A.	34.260	2	26	72
2.	Belgium	24,630	1	25	73
3.	U.K.	24,500	1	25	74
4.	Japan	34,210	2	36	62
5.	China	840	16	49	34
6.	India	460	27	27	46

Source: World Development Report (2002).

small scale sector was given special role for creating additional employment with low capital investment. A new thrust was given in favour of small units by the Industrial Policy statements of 1977 & 1990. During 1977, on the recommendation of Abid Hussain Committee, the Government of India has raised the investment on Plant and Machinery for small units and ancillaries from Rs. 75 lakhs to Rs. 3 croros and that for tiny units from Rs. 5 lakhs to Rs. 25 lakhs. Subsequently, the Government in 2000 has reduced the investment limit on plant and machinery from Rs. 3 crores to Rs. 1 crore.

A common classification is between traditional small scale industries and modern small scale industries. Traditional small scale industries include Khadi, Handloom, Village industries, Handicrafts, Sericulture, Coir etc. Modern small scale industries produce wide range of goods from comparatively simple items to sophisticated products such as Television sets, Electronic control system, various engineering products particularly, as ancillaries to the large industries. The traditional small Industries are highly labour intensive, while the modern small scale units make use of highly sophisticated machinery and equipment. For instance, during 1979-80 traditional small industires accounted for only 1394 of the total output for their share in total employment was 56%. In that year, total output of traditional small industries came to be Rs. 4420 crores and this output was produced with the employment of 133 workers, the average output of labour in traditional small industries was roughly Rs. 3,323.

As against this, the share of modern small industries in the total output of this sector was 74% in 1979-80 for their share of employment is only 33%. Obviously, these industrial units could be having higher labour productivity. For instance, in 1979-80 a total output of Rs. 24,885 Crores was produced by 78 Lakh workers in modern small scale industries — the average product of labour being Rs. 31,900/-.

Role of Small Scale Industries in Indian Economy

The small scale industrial sector which plays a pivotal role in the Indian Economy in terms of employment and growth has recorded a high rate of growth since Independence in spite of stiff competition from the large sector and not so-encouraging support from the Government. This is evidenced by the number of registered units which went up from 16,000 in 1950 to 33.7 lakh units in 2000-01. During the last decade alone, the small scale sector has progressed from the production of simple consumer goods to the manufacture of many sophisticated and precision products like electronics control system, micro-wave components, electro-medical equipment, TV etc.

The Government has been following a policy of reservation of items for exclusive development in the small-scale sector. At the time of the 1972 CENSUS of SMALL SCALE

INDUSTRIAL UNITS, there were 177 items in the reserved list. By 1983, the reserved list included 37 items for exclusive production in the small-scale sector. These units produce nearly 7500 commodities. The number of small-scale units have growth from 4.2 lakhs of 27 years, employment has grown from 4 million to 17.85 million and output has increased from Rs. 7200 crores to Rs. 5,78,470 crores. The following table records the employment and production in small scale sector in the country as a whole.

TABLE 2

Employment and Production in Small Scale Sector in India

		Production (Rs. Crores)			
Year	*No. of Units (in Lakhs)*	*(At current prices)*	*At (1993-94) Prices*	*Empl-oyment (in Lakhs)*	*Exports (Rs. Crores) at current Prices*
1973-74	4.20	7,200	—	39.7	393
1980-81	8,10	20,060	—	71.0	1,643
1990-91	19.50	1,55,340	1,55,340	125.3	9,100
1993-94	23.81	2,41,648	2,41,648	139.4	25,307
1994-95	25.71	2,98,886	2,66,054	146.6	29,068
1995-96	27.24	3,62,656	2,96,385	152.6	36,470
1996-97	28.57	4,11,858	3,29,935	160.0	39,249
1997-98	30.14	4,62,641	3,57,949	167.2	43,946
1998-99	31.21	5,20,650	3,85,296	171.6	43,979
1999-2000	32.25	5,72,887	4,16,736	178,5	53,975
2000-01	33.12	6,39,024	4,51,033	185.64	69,797
2001-02	34.42	6,90,316	4,78,456	192.23	NA
2002-03 (Projected)	35.72	7,42,021	5,14,292	199.65	NA

Source: Economic Survey (2002-03), GOI.

Despite the global and domestic recession, small scale Industries registered a higher growth rate than the overall industrial sector in terms of number of units, production, employment and exports. It may be observed that the number of SSl units increased from 4.20 Lakhs in 1973-74 to 35.72 Lakhs in 2002-03 (nearly 8/1/2 times). The estimated value of production at current prices has increased from Rs. 7,200 Crores in 1973-74 to Rs. 7,42,021 Crores in 2002-03 (more than 100 times). Likewise, total employment has increased from 39.7 lakhs in 1973-74 to 199.65 lakhs in Rs, 69,797 Crores in 2000-01 (nearly 177 times), although the figures are not available for the subsequent years. The SSI sector is one of the larger employers in the country, providing direct employment to more than 17 million persons, facilitating regional dispersal of industrial units and earning foreign exchange.

The Government of India has appointed a Committee under the Chairmanship of Dr. S.P. Gupta, Member, Planning Commission to study various developmental aspects relating to Small Scale Enterprises in India including the employment opportunities for the growing population. Its main recommendations ares (1) Whether India will be able to achieve its goal of generating 200 million jobs in the next two decades to solve the country's unemployment problems this is possible when it is able to concentrate on small and medium industries when are mostly in the unorganised sector; (2) It was also recommended for the easy availability of credit facilities as well as raising the productivity of the SSIs.

Here, it may not be out of place if international comparisons are made as far as the role of SSIs is concerned. It is a fact that even in a highly developed country like USA, nearly half of the workforce is employed in small firms, in Japan 78% jobs are in the small and medium sectors while in South Korea these sectors accounted for 69% of the total employment. The Committee's Report has pointed out that employment had nearly tripled in the country's small and medium sectors during the last two decades. If this trend continues, an additional 150-200 million jobs are likely to be created by these sectors by 2020.

The SSI Sector can brodly be devided into two sub-sectors:

(i) Modern Small Scale Industries

(ii) Traditional Industries.

The modern SSI Sector is akin to the large and medium scale industrial sector in terms of technology in use, production facilities, labour intensity, capital intensity etc., while the traditional industries include segments like handlooms, khadi and village industries handicrafts, sericulture, coir etc. These are generally artisan based, located mostly in rural or semi-uban areas, with nominal investment in plant and machinery.

Until 1991, the Indian Economy was practically isolated from the world economy, with stress being on indigenous production of manufactured goods and the domestic industries being protected from both internal and external competition. The protection from Internal competition was through a system of licensing and controls and that from external competition through restrictions on imports as well as high tariff barriers. In this background the entire industrial sector become inward-looking, with hardly any attention being paid to exports. While building up a industrial diversified high structure, it resulted in inadequate attention to upgradation of products and process technologies. R&D and cost reduction, resulting in lack of competitiveness.

Since 1991 the economy is gradually opened up and integrated to the global economy and the stress is on qualitative upgradation of the industrial structure and improving international competition of goods and services. The small scale sector has also responded well to the challenge of opening up the economy. The Government has been taking measures to promote growth and development of small scale enterprises. This includes provision of infrastructurel facilities, reservation of products for exclusive manufacture in the small scale sector, technology upgradation etc.

The following table records India's total exports as well as exports from SSI sector.

TABLE 3

Exports of SSI Sector in India

Year	*Total Exports (Rs. Crores)*	*Exports from SSI Sector (Rs. Crores)*	*SSI Exports as Percentage of total exports*
1951-52	716	Negligible	—
1971-72	1,608	155	9.6
1981-82	7,809	2,071	26.5
1991-92	44,040	13,883	31.5
1992-93	53,688	17,785	33.1
1993-94	69,547	25,307	36.4
1994-95	82,674	29,068	35.1
1995-96	1,06,353	36,470	34.2
1996-97	1,18,817	39,249	33.4
1997-96	1,26,286	44,442	35.2
1998-99	1,41,604	49,481	34.9
1999-2000	1,59,561	54,200	33.96
2000-01	2,03,571	69,797	34.28
2001-02	2,09,018	78.900	37.74

Source: Economic Survey (2002-03). GOI.

It may be observed that the share of SSI exports was very small in the initial stages. It gradually increased to about 27% in 1981-82. During 1990's, it has hovered around 30-35%. During 2001-02, the share of SSI sector's exports was almost 38%. Other details could be seen from Table 3.

A charge often made against the scale industries is that it cannot face world competition. But an analysis of its contribution to exports shows that the SSI sector's share in total exports was quite sizeable. This highlights the fact that a little more than one-third of total exports are contributed by the SSI sector. It may be noted that the rate of growth lavishly helped large industrial houses their contribution to exports is dismal, fall short in the performance of the SSI sector.

On the basis of the survey conducted to THE ANNUAL SURVEY OF INDUSTRIES (1994-95) these results are derived. With a Fixed Capital (PC) in Tiny Sector per employee of Rs. 11,391, it was possible to create Net Value Added (NVA) of the order of Rs. 35,638/-. This implies that to raise output (NAV) by one rupee investment in plant and machinery to the tune of Rs. 0.44 has to be made. This is a very favourable FC/NVA ratio in terms of growth. Similarly at a small investment of Rs. 11,391/-, it is possible to give employment to one person. Lower Capital employment ratio enable these tiny units to absorb nearly 16.6% of the total work force engaged in the factory sector. Likewise, in small scale sector the FC/NVA ratio was only 0.8 and Rs. 51,506/- were required in Fixed Capital to provide employment to one person.

Taking these two groups (Tiny sector and small sector) as comprising the total small scale sector, it was found out that with barely 3.5% of total investment in fixed capital, these units create about 13% of value added and 34% of total employment in the factory sector. There is no doubt that Net Value Added per employee in the small sector is low, for these units could be justified in terms of lower PC-/NVA ratio has also lower fixed capital per employee.

In contrast to the above picture, the large scale industrial units give a different picture. During 1994-95, large scale industrial units with a total fixed capital of Rs,1,71,466/- Crores (61% of the total capital) provided employment to only 16.27 lakh person (17.9% of total employment). The large scale units required an investment of Rs. 10,53,623/- in fixed Capital to create employment for one person. So far as small scale is concerned an investment in fixed capital of Rs. 31,928/- is required to employ one person. In other words, capital-employment ratio in the very large units is about 33 times higher than that of the small scale units. Similarly, capital employment ratio of large units is 10.8 times higher than the small scale units. Thus, one feels that the small scale units are justified on the basis of a lower capital employment ratio in a capital scarce country like India. Small scale units are also considered to be desirable from the point of view of growth since they have a low capital-output ratio as was indicated by FC/NVA.

The Annual Survey of Industries (1994-95) has listed two kinds of payments: (i) Wages to workers and (ii) Emoluments to employees; Workers include all persons employed directly or through any agency or wages. Employees include besides workers, all persons holding positions of supervision or Management or Administrative Officers or those engaged in the purchase of raw-materials etc. If we deduct from the employees the workers engaged in the manufacturing process, we are able to find the number of Supervisory/Managerial personnel. From the total employments, if we deduct wages we can obtain the payments made through Supervisory/ Managerial Personnel.

As per ASI, in the tiny sector, the proportion of workers and Supervisory/Managerial personnel was 86.14, this ratio changed to 78.22 for small enterprises, 77.32 for Medium Enterprises,' 73.27 for very large enterprises. In other words, in the factories in the higher capital range the proportion of supervisory Managerial cadres was higher since this cadre represents individuals with higher skills and capabilities and a relatively larger proportion of the total emoluments were received by them. In the tiny sector supervisory cadre received 24% of total emoluments, in the small sector they received about 35%, and in the large and very large enterprises, they received 39% and 41% respectively.

Small Enterprises and Poverty Level in India

As per ASI data the average annual wage per worker in 1994-95 was Rs. 12,889/-for the tiny sector, Rs. 18,853/- for small sector, Rs. 29,737/-for medium sector and Rs. 46,383/- for large sector and Rs. 57,205/- for very large sector.

The Expert Group of the Planning Commission in 1994-95, the Urban poverty line has been revised to Rs,1626/- per annum taking the family average size at 5, whereas the annual expenditure worked out to be Rs.19,510/-. Comparing it with the annual wages received per worker in the tiny sector at Rs. 12,889/- one reaches the conclusion that workers engaged in the tiny sector had received only 66% wages as against that required to keep the family above the poverty line. When compared to this, wages in the small sector per worker were Rs.18,853/- which is nearly 97% of the total expenditure to keep them above the poverty line. Of course, the analysis given above is based on two assumptions. (i) Workers, families are single earner families; (ii) Size of the family consists of a total 5 persons.

However, it may be noted that since the coverage size per worker in the medium sector, large sector and very large sector is higher than the annual expenditures require to keep them above the poverty line. It can be concluded that 64% of the workers employed in the factory are living above the poverty line.

Distribution of Net Value Added (NVA) in Indian Industries (1994-95)

The NVA per employee was Rs.25,683/- in tiny sector rising to Rs.64,148/- in the small sector, Rs.1,75,985/- in the large sector and further to Rs. 2,27,068/~ in the very large sector. It is the Net Value Added which is to be distributed among workers as wages, payments to supervisory/ managerial personnel, rent, interest and profits.

The data received that the share of workers in NVA as wage a was 43.4% in the tiny sector, 23% for the small sector and 19% in the large scale sector and only 17% in the very large sector. Emoluments for supervisory personnel were above 14% in the tiny sector and 12.3% for small sector and in the range of 12-13% for medium, large and very large sectors.

From the foregoing analysis, it becomes evident that as capital size of factories increases, the share of income of the propertied classes, in the form of rent, Interest and profit goes up. The share of the propertied classes was 43% in case of the tiny sector, went up to about 65%, in the case of small and medium units, and was of the order of 69% and 71% for large and very large sectors respectively.

Some important measures are to be undertaken to revitalize the SSI Sector. Some of them are as follows:

1. Normally,Tiny sector is neglected in the provision of credit facilities. Special efforts should be made to extend more credit facilities at relatively cheaper interest rates by banks and other financial institutions. In this connection, Nayak Commission's recommendations are to be followed.
2. Small Scale Sector should not be allowed to remain at the mercy of market forces but should be suitably

strengthened with more resources, technical know-how and preferential purchase mechanism to enable it to grow at a faster rate. New techniques are to be introduced wherever they are feasible.

3. Instead of emphasizing competition between small sector and large sector, it would be more desirable to foster competition within the small sector.
4. State should not only provide for fixed capital requirements of SSIs but also should provide the working capital 30 that production con be carried on without interruption.
5. According to Annual Survey of Industries (ASI), a small effort by way of providing better credit and marketing facilities, the SSI Sector in India can lift 17% of the workers employed in this sector above the poverty line.
6. The SSI Sector has to face challenges of competition from outside the country, in the context of globalization and WTO regulations. This challenge has to be faced.
7. Of late, Small Enterprises are increasingly owned by women. Necessary arrangements may be made for turning out better women entrepreneurs.

New Economic Policy Reforms or Liberalisation Policies

The salient features of the New Economic Policy which has come into vogue in 1991 are as follows:

(i) The public sector is to receive backseat and the free market economy is gradually favoured.

(ii) Towards this end, a policy of closing down 'Sick' public sector Industrial units has been announced. The related policy of disinvestment has also been announced.

(iii) More free entry of the private sector in industries.

(iv) Freer entry of foreign capital and investments, including foreign technology transfere.

(v) Freer imports following improvement in foreign exchange reserves situation.

(vi) No upper limit for monopoly business.

(vii) Opening up channels for utilising the 'black money' which was largely the creation of 'Control-permit raj', into fruitful investments, and that too, without either explanation or asking any questions.

As an offshoot of some of these measures, banks have been permitted to close down branches other than rural areas as well as to swap unremunerative branches or those in remote areas.

Prof. S.P. Gupta, Member, Planning Commission who headed a Committee on India Vision 2020, has submitted its report to the Govt. of India, a *few* months ago. According to him, small scale industries have a vital role to play in the country's economy as far as creation of new Jobs is concerned. He says that availability *of* credit should *be improved* and *also* the overall productivity to be raised. Prof. Gupta pointed out that employment had tripled in the country's small and medium sectors in the last two decades. If this trend continued, an additional 150-200 million Jobs would be created by these sectors by 2020. The Gupta Committee pointed out that the public sector would continue to shed jobs, while the private organised sector which currently accounted for 2.5% of all jobs had only modest potential for creating new Jobs. Even if this sector were to grow at 30% per annum, in five years it would contribute less than 1% to the growth of work force.

REFERENCES

1. Cortes Mariluz *et al.*, (1987) *Success in small and Medium Scale Enterprises: The Evidence From Columbia,* Oxford University Press London/Washington.
2. Desai Ashok and Nisha Taneja (1990) *The Role of Small and Medium Scale Manufacturing Industries in Industrial Development: The Experience of Selected Asian Countries.*
3. Dhar R.N. and H.F. Lyall (1961), *The Role of Small Enterprises in Indian Economic Development,* Asian Publishing House, Mumbai.
4. Katherine Marton (1986), *Multinationals, Technology, and Industrialisation Implications and Impact in Third World Countries,* Lexington Books, Toronto, Canada.
5. Little IMD et al. (1987), *Small Manufacturing Enterprises: A Comparative Analysis of India and other Economics,* Oxford University Press, New York.
6. Rauce M.Y. and M.B. Yaw (1983), *Managing the Development of Agro-Food Industries in the 1980's,* OECD, Paris.
7. Sreevastava, U.K. and S. Vatsala (1991); *Agro-Processing Strategy Acceleration for Export,* Oxford University Press, Delhi.
8. Suri, K,B. (Ed.) (1000), *Small Scale Enterprises in Industrial Development the Indian Experience,* Sage Pub lications, New Delhi.
9. Brahmananda, P.R. and Panchamukhi, V.R. (Eds.) (1987), *The Development Process of the Indian Economy,* Bombay, Himalaya Publishing House.
10. Schumacher, EF (1973), *Small is Beautiful,* London, Blond Brigges.
11. T.S., Papola, (1982), *Rural Industrilisational Approachs and Potential,* Himalaya Publishing House, Bombay.
12. J.C. Sandesara; *Industrial Policy and Planning* (1992), Sage Publications, New Delhi.
13. B. Satyanarayan, *India's Trade with Asia and the Far East Countries,* B.R., Publishing Corporation, New Delhi, (1986).
14. B. Satyanaryan, (Edited), *A Comparative Study of Foreign Direct Investment in India and China Problems and Prospects,* Himalaya Publishing House, (1996).
15. B. Satyanarayan, (Edited), *Social Sciences and Planning for Sustainable Development,* Himalaya Publishing House, (1998).

16. B. Satyanarayan (Edited Jointly), *Essays in Political Economy,* Concept Publishing Co., New Delhi, (1999).

17. B. Satyanarayan (Edited) *Growth, Industrialisation and New Economic Reforms in India,* Concept Pub.Co., New Delhi (2001).

18. *Economic Surveys,* G.O.I. 1997-98, 1999-2000 and 2000-01.

24

Panchayat Raj Institutions and Economic Development

It is a fact that more than 80 countries in the World to-day have a per capita income lower than a decade ago. Inequality between countries has increased tremendously over the decade of 1990s. According to the "Human Development Report" of 1999, the income gap between a fifth of World's population living in the richest countries and a fifth in the poorest, increased from 60 to 1 in 1990 to 74 to 1 in 1997. This inequality between the developed and developing countries is likely to worsen as globalization proceeds.

The concept of Human Development which was pioneered by the UNDP in 1990 attempts to go beyond per capita income in measuring the well-being of people. This it has done so by giving the health and educational status of the citizens of each country equal importance in the measure of well-being. According to the latest Human Development Report (2001), when it comes to progress in life expectancy, adult literacy, school enrollment and per capita GNP (the four indicators that constitute the Human Development Index), India's-progress in 1990 has taken it to the category of countries with "Medium Human Development".

Hunger and Malnutrition could cost the World about $

500 billions a year. The undernourished people in the World for 2003-04 were 852 millions, of which 815 were in the Developing World, 28 millions in the transition economies and 9 millions in the industrialized countries. Some of these details are shown in the following table:

TABLE 1

World's Hungry People: (In Millions)

SI.No.	*Country*	*1990-92*	*1995-97*	*2000-02*
	(1)	(2)	(3)	(4)
(i)	India	215	203	221.1
(ii)	China	193.5	145.6	141.1
(iii)	Bangladesh	39.2	50.4	42.5
(iv)	Ethiopia	NA	35.8	31.3

Statement of the Problem

A developing country like India is still faced with quite a large section of population which is not only illiterate and below poverty line, but also either employed, un-employed or non-employed. The main focus of Indian Planning so far has been on growth and social justice. The main reason as to why a large chunk of this country's population is suffering still from a sub-standard or sub-subsistence modicum of living is that no systematic thought has been given to provide the basic consumer's essentials to the target groups. It was expected that special employment and income generation measures would serve the purpose. Scarce resources which could have been utilized for creating assets, which in turn could have secured a continuous flow of employment and reduction of poverty in a systematic manner, have had to be diverted for the creation of adhoc opportunities of employment or poverty relief measures or welfare programmes. As a matter of fact, the major flaw in Indian Planning is that a relevant production spectrum has never been designed on a longer term basis to achieve reasonable degree of consumption, equalitarianism through the choices of appropriate rules and techniques, incomes and wages policies, employment and man-power planning.

As a matter of fact, when theories of development relevant to a mixed economy undergoing transition from a low level of development to a state of advancement may be spread over a long period of 75-100 years. After all in a country's span of life, this is not at all a longer period. The Perspective Plan Model visualized by both Mahalanobis and Pittambarpanth was hardly 15-20 years only. The strategy of National Development for underdeveloped countries should aim at achieving the standards in terms of income, literacy, education, sanitation, health etc., prevalent in the middle level countries, if not the highly developed countries like U.S.A.

Planning and Economic Reforms

The Government should evolve policy measures, so that its output is carefully and preferentially used. For example, electricity will have to be provided to agricultural sectors at a subsidized rate, whereas it should be provided at a relatively more cost to the industries providing the non-priority sector groups, which may also be known as non-essential commodities. Likewise, within the industrial sector, Small Scale and Cottage Industries will have to be provided at a relatively low cost. In a similar way, all the inputs to all the priority industries will have to be ensured at a relatively low cost. Incidentally, this type of planning and strategy will also provide large number of employment opportunities to a large number of unemployed people, both skilled and unskilled, rural and urban. As far as technology is concerned, we should not blindly go in for high capital intensive techniques in all the lines of production. Of course, we have to adopt latest techniques, which are available all over the World in some selected areas like defence, satellites, tele-communications, radars, hardware, software, etc. But this tendency should be curbed in the field of consumer goods including durables. Wherever these consumer durables are produced, imported and consumed, they have to be heavily taxed. On the other hand, a country like ours in the name of New Economic Policy and Liberalization, we are exactly following the other way round. Likewise, we are also now inviting the foreign investment with a red carpet. Foreign investment will be restricted to the priority areas only. The Central Government will have to have a long term and perspective planning covering the basic areas and needs of the society. It should not compete with the State Governments.

Planning in India

Free trade in India's agricultural commodities may lead to a massive transfer of purchasing power from urban/rural consumers to farmers. Considering the fact, for nearly four decades till 1991 witnessed high relative production of industrial products, this step probably looks reasonable. As a matter of fact, China did effect such a transfer in 1978 when it opened up internal trade in agricultural items. But China could forcibly control any urban uprising. This is not possible in India with its democratic background. What the Indian Government can do is to bring in more agricultural items into its Public Distribution System at least in the short run. This may cost the Government a little bit more.

Critics argue that there are likely to be gains in exporting processed food items from India. This is of course true. In most processed food items Indian prices are way below the US levels, when the commodity is domestically produced. But these gains would accrue to the industrial and not the agricultural sector. The issue is here not efficiency but the resistance to change to the costs of structural adjustments. No doubt efficiency calculations would show the need to re-orient Indian agriculture in the right direction. One such change would be large scale farming to obtain productivity increases. But none of the present reforms show any such concerns dominate policy making. Given the fragmented nature of Indian agriculture one does not see where the productivity increase is going to come from. In the long run, rising agricultural prices could lead to an increase in wages in the agriculturai sector and arrest the current unsustainable population pressure in urban areas.

Two decades ago, in rural India, out of every hundred families, 31% were landless. To-day the figure has gone up to 41%. The following table shows the changes that have taken place between various sectors in the economy.

TABLE 2

Contribution in GDP (Percentage) in India

S.No.	*Item/Sector*	*1970s*	*2003-04*
1.	Agriculture	42.8%	22.19%
2.	Industry	22.8%	26.9%
3.	Services	34.4%	51.0%
	Total	100%	100%

The pertinent questions which would be raised and addressed are as follows:

(i) What are the factors which are causing the price escalation and rise in the fiscal expenditure. How to reduce the un-productive and non-developmental expenditure?

(ii) How to raise the real wage level of the working population;

(iii) How to increase the over all employment opportunities;

(iv) How to reduce the poverty levels in the country;

(v) What means are required to raise the over all living standards;

(vi) Austerity at all levels are to be strictly followed. Conspicuous consumption by all the persons and organizations are to be eschewed. Better standards are to be setup.

The Prevailing India's Economic Scenario

When the ongoing economic reforms were initiated in 1991 a feeling was created that these reforms would be reaped from the beginning of the new millennium. Even after 55 years of India's Independence, the present picture of the country is as follows:

(i) Nearly 300 millions of our people are still illitcrate;

(ii) Around 30-40% of our people are poor or below the poverty line;

(iii) Around 1,75,000 villages of the country do not have potable drinking water within the vicinity of 1.5 Kms and thousands of our villages do not have even approach roads;

(iv) More than 80% of the students are dropouts by the time they reach 8th standard and 50% invariably fail at the S.S.C. level;

(v) Social and economic disparities have further widened and the new economic order was aggravated the situation beyond redemption unless it is controlled and regulated;

(vi) Explosion of population and fast degradation of

environment have endangered the very survival of the people as well as the country;

(vii) The average per capita income in terms of 1996 dollars is as follows:

(a) India ... $380;

(b) South Asia ... $ 380;

(c) Sub-Saharan Africa ... $ 490;

(d) East Asia & Pacific ... $ 890;

(e) High Income Countries ... $ 25,870.

25

India and China: A Comparison*

China was proclaimed as People's Republic in Peking on October 1st, 1941 under Mao Tse-tung. On October 26, 1971 China was admitted as a member of the UN, displacing nationalist China (Taiwan). It is the most populous country in the world and the third largest in area. The total population of China is 1304 millions, while the overall literacy rate is nearly 82%. It is made up of 22 Provinces, 5 autonomous regions and 4 Municipalities. Nearly 2/3rds of the territory is either mountainous or desert; only 1/10th is cultivated. The eastern half of China is one of the world's biggest watered lands.

China is essentially an agricultural country. The main crops are rice, tea, tobacco, sugarcane, jute, soybean, groundnut and hemp. The main forest products are teak and ting oil. At least 80 million Chinese farmers in 1984 were in search of various opportunities of employment. Their incomes are less than 1/3rd of city dwellers. The migrants believe that they have nothing to lose. Their cheap labour has become a major factor in keeping China's economic growth at 13% annually. Now, most urban construction workers, garbage collectors, street sweepers, maids, bicycle repairmen, shoe sellers and

* Also appeared in Business Vision, Vol. 1, No. 3, July-Sept. 2005.

popcorn vendors are migrants from rural areas. Most migrants live as cheaply as possible in the cities and send money home that spurs development in the villages. According to a survey, the average income was equivalent to $ 50 a year per family without migrant members and $ 147 of those if some one was working in the city.

In 2000, the per capita net income of rural dwellers in China and the per capitable disposal income of urban recipients was 2253 Yuan and 6280 Yuan, respectively, which increased by 4.7% and 5.7% annually in real terms. Since then the number of people below poverty line in the rural areas decreased drastically. The objectives set for the Seventh Plan (1994-2000) to help 80 million people out of poverty were basically attained. The Tenth Five Year Plan for national economic and social development (2001-2005) listed five guiding principles. They have set their target at 7% rate of growth during this plan.

The per head living area for China's urban residents has increased from 3.6 square meters in 1978 to 7.3 square meters in 1993. In the countryside since the peasants' living standards have improved, the expense for home building has increased constantly. The per capita expense on housing in 1993 was 29 times of that in 1978. Big household articles in 1970's - bicycle, watch and sewing machine — have already been replaced by three new ones - color TV, washing machine, and refrigerator. Likewise, the telephone ownership rate was 0.38% in 1978 and in 1993 the rate was 2.5% which was equivalent to the average level of countries across the world where per capita income is US dollars 900. The tele density now in China is 10:5.

The principal industries are cotton and woolen mills, iron, leather and electrical equipment. The chief minerals are coal, manganese, iron-ore, zinc, gold, silver, tungsten, mercury, antimony and tin. The petroleum industry is gradually but steadily growing.

In China foreign trade is more or less acting as growth engine rising from 15% in 1980 to over 50% of the GDP today. China is very competitive in legible exports (manufactures). The booming current account surplus in China is due to the big diaspora, which is traditionally more entrepreneurial.

China has a very strong political commitment to reforms thereby showing greater urgency in privatizing a number of State Enterprises and also lowered trade barriers. In the pre-reform period China made much greater investment in the social infrastructure such as health,-education and agricultural infrastructure thus eliminating absolute poverty.

China has an aggressive FDI policy for attracting investment in the labour-intensive manufacturing sector in Coastal Special Economic Zones (SEZ) insulated from the domestic policy environment.

India and China—Comparative Study

India and China have established their Republics more or less at less at the same time. Both the countries have adopted Five Year Plans, although with different political setups. India's policy is governed by the Centre in Delhi. This is not so in China, where provinces are free to make situational adjustments leading to national advantage. India's restrictive policies owing to several constraints are a serious drag on the economic growth that needs to be drastically changed.

Even then, some similarities are striking between these two countries. China and India are amongst the five biggest countries in the world in terms of area, geographical diversity, population, market-size and economy measured in their purchasing power parity. They both are ancient countries. Both the countries were colonized and attained Independence in the mid twentieth century. They pursued socialist models of development before opening up gradually, China from 1978 onwards and India from 1991 onwards. China and India are presently the fastest growing major economies of the world, although majority of the population continues to be dependent on agriculture. The State and Centre continue to dominate economic activity in both the countries; the role of private enterprises is expanding fast. A rapid economic growth has widened regional economic disparities in them.

They both face serious fiscal problems and growing foreign and domestic debts. However, much of India's public sector deficit has been absorbed directly by the government, whereas China has relied heavily on banking system to fund the deficit. Therefore, while India has fiscal deficits, China's banking system has more non-performing assets.

There are major differences too. China has a very strong political commitment to reform, while India hasn't. Thus, China has shown far greater urgency in privatizing and closing a large number of state enterprises, while India's privatization programme has floundered. Economic decentralization has proceeded at a much faster pace in China, with local governments having an effective economic strength and decision-making power, whereas India's specialized economic control is loosening gradually.

In the pre-reform period, China made greater investment in the social infrastructure such as health, education and agriculture infrastructure than India, thereby eliminating absolute poverty. India, on the other hand, under-invested in social and agricultural infrastructure and currently has the single largest mass of poor people in the world.

China had an aggressive FDI policy for attracting investment in the labour-intensive manufacturing sector.

Initially it encouraged FDI in high technology and infrastructure sectors. While China invested huge amounts of public funds in developing its infrastructure, India's economic reforms cutback public investment on the infrastructure, relying on private investment that has been slow to fructify.

While China is a closed economy run by a tightly knit Communist Party, India is an open democratic society, with an independent judiciary and the press. China has overt political stability. India has a long history of political power through ballot box at both Central and State levels, an overt history which nevertheless underscores the inherent stability of its political institutions.

The Following Table Gives Data for the Economic Variables Both for India and China

S.No.	*Item*	*India (2001-02)*	*China (2002)*
(1)	(2)	(3)	(4)
1.	Population (Millions)	1,000	1300
2.	Poverty ratio	29%	7%
3.	GDP ($ billion)	510.2	1232.7
4.	GDP growth rate	4.40%	8.09%
5.	Share of GDP - Agriculture	22.7%	14.6%
6.	Share of GDP- Industry	26.6%	51.7%
7.	Share of GDP - Services	50.7%	33.7%
8.	Volume of Trade ($ billions)	157	623
9.	Foreign Direct Investment ($ Billion)	4	53

Source: World Bank "India at a Glance and "China at a Glance".

It may be seen that the G.D.P. of China, which was about 1.2 times that of India in 1982, had grown to 2.6 times in 2002 to that of India. In terms of impact of the economic growth on poverty, China in 2002 had lifted 400 million people out of poverty and its poverty ratio had declined to 4.6%. Over the same period, the poverty ratio in India had declined from 36% to 29% only.

China and the Global Scenario

Rapid industrialization of China on a gigantic scale was triggered after the tour of the southern provinces by the late Deng Xiaoping in 1992 when he gave the ahead for the transformation of the region. Since then there is no looking back and the rapid growth of industries in China has sent shockwaves through the manufacturing world. Since the financial crisis of 1997, the economies of South East Asia have seen the investments in mass manufacturing go north towards China.

The great industrial transformation in China has brought up a number of salient issues relevant for global manufacturing, which will remain important for some years to come. Global manufacturing is being shaped by the happenings in China. Entire value chains in many industries are being reconfigured and realigned. China's accession to the World Trade Organization (WTO) is accelerating these processes.

Index

■■■